Praise for Confronting the Pope of Suspicion:

"It's not that complicated. Replace divine law with pop psychology and disaster follows. [Confronting the Pope of Suspicion] connects the dots between Amoris Laetitia, Carl Rogers, theological dissent, and sexual chaos in the Church. A short but profound read." —**Jennifer Roback Morse,** author of *The Sexual State: How Elite Ideologies Are Destroying Lives and Why the Church Was Right All Along*

"John Gravino presents here a sober, thoroughly documented, and powerfully argued case that the sexual abuse of children became an epidemic among Catholic clergy because relativistic psychology replaced Biblical morality in the training of priests."

"One of the most important Catholic commentators today."

"A brilliant Catholic philosopher and theologian." —**John Zmirak,** author of *The Politically Incorrect Guide to Catholicism*

"Y'all, about 99% of this lemon papacy s dissected, described, and set in context by Mr. Gravino."
—**Patrick Coffin**, The Patrick Coffin Show

CONFRONTING THE POPE OF SUSPICION

The Key to Church Reform

John Gravino

Copyright © 2019 by John A. Gravino, III
All rights reserved.

Unless otherwise noted, Scripture passages have been taken from the Revised Standard Version of the Bible, copyright © 1946, 1952, and 1971 the Division of Christian Education of the National Council of the Churches of Christ in the United States of America. Used by permission. All rights reserved.

To Our Lady of Paris—to the rebuilding of that glorious monument to her—a monument to the marriage of human soul and Holy Spirit—a monument to the Christian spirit of the medieval age, to the marriage of faith and reason. Dedicated to the rebuilding of that temple—and dedicated to the rebuilding of its spirit in our hearts.

CONTENTS

THE SUMMIT

13

MEET THE MASTERS OF SUSPICION

15

CLOSE ENCOUNTERS WITH CARL ROGERS

27

THE SEXUAL ABUSE OF MINORS

31

THE JOHN PAUL REFORM

37

POPE FRANCIS

42

AMORIS LAETITIA—THE LANGUAGE PROBLEM

45

CAN WE REFORM THE POPE OF SUSPICION?

67

POSTSCRIPT 2021: AMORIS LAETITIA —TROJAN HORSE FOR GAY FASCISM

75

BIBLIOGRAPHY

98

NOTES

107

PREFACE

It's the "Year of Reflection on *Amoris Laetitia*" according to a decree by Pope Francis. In truth, it's more like a year of promotion and implementation than anything else. What a disaster for the Church and for souls. I originally published *Confronting the Pope of Suspicion* in 2019 as an e-book to warn people about the dangers of this papal document. And so, in an effort to facilitate this project of genuine reflection, I am redoubling my efforts to warn you, yet again, of the dangers lurking within *Amoris Laetitia*. Hence, this new, expanded *paperback* edition of *Confronting the Pope of Suspicion*. The new edition contains the entirety of the original text with only minor changes. What's new is a five-thousand-word postscript that describes the important developments that have taken place since my book was first published. In a year that is certain to be filled with fawning propaganda, I offer this little book as a necessary corrective.

Four cardinals tried to warn us, but nobody listened[1]: *Amoris Laetitia* is poisoning our seminaries and our seminarians with its moral relativism. In this year of *implementation*, the plan is to destroy our local parishes as well. Of course, the cheerleaders for *Amoris Laetitia* wouldn't describe it like that. They would call it *modernization*. Indeed, it is modern to grant approval to sexual sin—not Christian, but modern. If *Amoris Laetitia* takes hold of the Church, what we will get is a brand new church, founded, no longer on the teachings of Christ and the Apostles, but on the propaganda of modernity, which the modernists themselves call "science."

This new church seeks its salvation, not in the approval of God, but of men. And therein lies the darkest secret of *Amoris Laetitia*. Because *Amoris Laetitia* sets aside the Commandments of God and grants permission to all the world to indulge its favorite sexual sins, the world will richly reward this new church of Bergoglio. And it will come at the expense of the true Church. Consider for a moment the dangerous prospect of an alliance, formal or not, between an apostate hierarchy and the secular powers of state and media. The likely consequence will be the disenfranchisement of the true Church in a dystopic mirroring of the situation in China where only the state-recognized unholy church enjoys any rights or protections, and all the members of the true Church become organ donors.[2]

In the short tract that follows, I explain briefly the essential intellectual history of *Amoris Laetitia,* and I show how I came to these dark realizations and how they are coming true all around the world, most especially in Germany. The best defense against this mass apostasy is to tell the truth. I hope this little book will help you to do just that.

❇ ❇ ❇

> *"For the lips of a priest should guard knowledge, and men should seek instruction from his mouth, for he is the messenger of the Lord of hosts. But you have turned aside from the way; you have caused many to stumble by your instruction; you have corrupted the covenant of Levi, says the Lord of hosts, and so I make you despised and abased before all the people...."*

> MALACHI 2:7–9

THE SUMMIT

Tackling Sexual Abuse in a Divided Church

When Pope emeritus Benedict's letter on sexual abuse was published, the responses from Catholic pundits ranged from enthusiastic approbation to derisive opprobrium.[3] Some commenters correctly noted that Benedict's analysis bore no resemblance to that which came out of last February's Vatican abuse summit.[4] This raises an urgent question. Can the Church, divided as it is, ever implement effective reform if it cannot agree on the causes of the most damaging Church scandal in centuries?

The question is not an academic one. According to a recent report by Dr. Paul Sullins, sexual abuse by clergy may be on the rise once again.[5] This is just another dispiriting indicator that the crisis is not over, and, despite seventeen years of pressure from front-page news coverage, the Church has yet to enact effective reform. The failure to come up with a plan for effective reform in all these seventeen years since the scandal exploded in 2002 points to a failure to see the problem for what it is. The purpose of this little tract is to persuade you that Benedict was exactly right in his analysis of the scandal. At its roots, the crisis in the Church is intellectual and philosophical.[6] It is the story of a theological crisis that ended in sexual abuse. Here is that story.

❋ ❋ ❋

MEET THE MASTERS OF SUSPICION

John Paul the Great pinpointed the origin of the theological crisis in his much-discussed-but-rarely-read magnum opus *The Theology of the Body.* He mentions three European thinkers whom Paul Ricoeur identified as the masters of suspicion.[7] What Freud, Marx, and Nietzsche shared in common according to Ricoeur was a deep suspicion about a theologically informed understanding of human nature. According to the "masters," these Bible-inspired ideas were primitive, superstitious, and inimical to human happiness. What they mounted, in effect, was a grand psychological critique of Christianity. And because Ricoeur was European, it is understandable that he would single out three European thinkers for the distinction.

But America produced one of its own masters of suspicion who, like his European counterparts, was inspired by the romantic era of the nineteenth century to issue a direct challenge to the hegemony of Christian principles. In his essay "Self-Reliance," Ralph Waldo Emerson sums up the romantic, individualistic spirit of these nineteenth-century heretics:

> I remember an answer which when quite young I was prompted to make to a valued adviser, who was wont to importune me with the dear old doctrines of the church. On my saying, What have I to do with the sacredness of traditions, if I live wholly from within? my friend suggested,—"But these impulses may be from below, not from above." I replied, "They do not seem to me to be such; but if I am the Devil's child, I will live then from the Devil." *No law can be sacred to me but that of my nature. Good and bad are but names very readily transferable to that or this; the only right is what is after my constitution, the only wrong what is against it."*[8]

This was a direct assault on a standard Christian doctrine, well known in the Victorian era, as Emerson admits. It was the denial of Original Sin —the idea that humanity was burdened by a fallen and disordered human nature. The doctrine goes all the way back to the Bible and is associated with St.

Confronting the Pope of Suspicion

Paul, though it is present in other places, notably in most if not all of the Epistles. But it is also present in the words of Christ, himself, who teaches that impurity comes from within the heart (Mk. 7: 18–23).

In a Christianity marked by disagreement and disunity, the doctrine of Original Sin represented a rare point of consensus. Hence the universal familiarity with some of its characteristic corollaries—our impure hearts give rise to impure passions—the seven deadly sins.

The doctrine of our fallen nature formed the backbone of what John Paul called the Bible's moral psychology.[9] It is the Bible's very own version of the natural law. Moral prescriptions and prohibitions flow logically from psychological facts of our nature, specifically that our consciousness is infected by certain disordered passions that lead us into sin and immorality. It follows from these psychological facts that such troublesome passions should be discouraged in some way. In the words of St. Peter: "Abstain from the passions of the flesh that wage war against your soul" (1Pt 2:11).

But this is good advice only if the Bible got the facts right about Original Sin and humanity's disordered nature. That is what Emerson was denying in the quote above, and the same with all the masters of suspicion. It was their primary complaint about Christianity, namely, that it got human nature all wrong.[10] And if the Church was wrong about humanity's corrupt nature, it was also wrong to teach people to deny a nature that was in fact innocent. The masters of suspicion were issuing a direct challenge to the Church's ascetical ethic. Enter Nietzsche:

> The ascetic ideal, with its sublime moral cult, with its brilliant and irresponsible use of the emotions for holy purposes, has etched itself on the memory of mankind terribly and unforgettably. I can think of no development that has had a more pernicious effect upon the health of the race, and especially the European race, than this. *It may be called, without exaggeration, the supreme disaster in the history of European man's health. . . . [T]he ascetic priest has corrupted man's mental health wherever he has held sway...*"[11]

Not only is Christian self-denial pointless, according to Nietzsche, it is psychologically harmful, a point that would be taken up later by Sigmund Freud. Freud brought to this discussion the rigorous empirical tools of the scientific method. He brought forth clinical evidence from his psychological practice which suggested that Christian ascetical principles were harmful. Had science discovered that the Bible was wrong in its moral psychology? Freud was saying so. The new science of psychology was issuing a direct challenge to the authority of Christian doctrine and revelation. It certainly wasn't the first run-in between faith and science.

Freud offered a powerful variation on the old heresy of Pelagianism—call it scientific Pelagianism or psychological Pelagianism. It argued from *empirical* grounds that the ascetical life of the Church did not lead to an enlightened state of being as the Church taught. Christian holiness was a fraud, the pursuit of which brought individuals into conflict with their own nature. It was a conflict that never had a happy ending. It did not lead to a transcendent state or a higher spiritual plane of being. Instead it shackled individuals to miserable and hopeless inner conflicts that uniformly ended badly—to a warped psychological state. It wasn't human fulfillment as the Church taught. It was the destruction of human happiness and human potential. Freud explains in general terms the dire consequences of this "excessive" self-denial: "If more is demanded of a man, a revolt will be produced in him or a neurosis, or he will be made unhappy."[12] And the problem according to Freud was most acute in the case of sex:

> "Present-day civilization makes it plain that it will only permit sexual relationships on the basis of a solitary, indissoluble bond between one man and one woman, and that it does not like sexuality as a source of pleasure in its own right and is only prepared to tolerate it because there

> is so far no substitute for it as a means of propagating the human race. . . . *Only the weaklings have submitted to such an extensive encroachment upon their sexual freedom....*"[13]

So if one's sexual desires violate the norms of Christian morality—so what? Only a "weakling" would worry. Freud used a psychological argument to discredit Christian morality. But if the morality that shaped Western civilization for two-thousand years led only to neurosis, as Freud claimed, what then should take its place? What should guide our moral reasoning? Emerson provided the formula: It was my own "nature" that should be my guide. If I had a desire for the opposite sex, then that is what I should pursue. If the *same* sex, then that is what I should pursue. My conscience, at least as far as sex was concerned, was no longer to be formed by a moral law that paid no attention to my particular passions and desires. In the eyes of many, psychology had become the champion of a new sexual liberation which promised greater freedom, happiness, and personal growth. But like the promises of a certain ancient serpent, the promises of the new psychology would prove empty and false.

The Power of the Psychological Critique—Theological Implications

Freud's psychological Pelagianism threw a gigantic monkey wrench into the moral economy of the Church. The moral laws concerning sexuality were a serious matter—you could go to hell for breaking some of them. Eternal damnation represented easily the most persuasive argument against certain sins. But Freud's psychological critique cast doubt on these claims. For the Bible also taught that only the holy and the perfect, those who had been conformed to the image of Christ, could enter heaven (Heb. 12:14). Certainly psychological impairment was incompatible with the holiness and perfection necessary for the beatific vision. Certainly Jesus was not a neurotic. If we were meant by God to be conformed to the image and likeness of his Son, then sexual repression and mental disorder were out of the question. Psychological disorder was incompatible with the holiness and perfection that were necessary for salvation and eternal happiness.

Moreover, if the teachings of Christ were intended to bring human nature to perfection, but instead, it could be demonstrated that those teachings were psychologically harmful, then Christ could not be the God who is all- knowing and powerful. And we would not be under any obligation to follow teachings that made false promises of healing and perfection, but instead produced quite the opposite.

The scientific study of human nature posed a real threat to Christianity. As the sciences progressed in their understanding of human nature, would their findings refute the biblical claims that Christianity presented an authentic spiritual path to human perfection and fulfillment? It's a thorny problem for the Church really. The Church claims infallible knowledge of human nature that is at least, in part, derived from divine revelation. And a new science was claiming to have empirical evidence that refutes that biblical understanding. Whom should we believe?

The appearance of psychology as a new science and academic discipline posed an existential threat to the priesthood, as Carl Jung observed in his book *Modern Man in Search of a Soul*. In the event of a spiritual crisis, to whom should one turn—the priest or the therapist? This was the question Jung asked at the end of that book. Increasingly, Jung observed, people were staying away from "the minister of the church ... [due to] his lack of psychological knowledge and insight...."[14]

Those were Jung's words in 1933. And they presaged a revolution in theology. If ministers were going to be of help to their flocks, they would need to educate themselves in the new field of psychology. By 1978, before John Paul II ever ascended to the papal throne, the revolution was complete, and the obituary of orthodoxy had already been written.

The Seismic Legacy of the Psychological Critique

Encyclopedias will tell you that the birth of psychology took place in 1878. And on the centenary of this most fateful event, *The New Catholic Encyclopedia* fittingly published its 17th volume entitled *Change in the Church*, bequeathing to posterity an historical record of the theological revolution that rocked the Church. It is the respected Jesuit historian Joseph Becker who points us to this volume—in particular, to the article on vows ("Vow: Practice and Theology," pp.696–699). At the end of his two-volume history of the Jesuits, Becker admits that his history is incomplete and that more needed to be written about how the theology of religious vows had been radically altered in the sixties. He suggests that the encyclopedia article would make an excellent guidepost for such a history.[15] What does that article say?

> "First, there has been a reversal in the relationship between canonical legislation and the theology of religious life. Prior to Vatican II the theology of religious life in general, and of the vows in particular, was almost wholly derived from Canon Law. *The Council's invitation to religious to renew their institutes led to wide experimentation, much of it contrary to common law and custom.*"[16]

That brief statement speaks volumes. First, it tells us that the breaking of religious vows was widespread. How widespread exactly? The introductory paragraph calls these "experimenters" "the progressive majority."[17] That's in 1978. Second, it attempts to justify these obvious betrayals of orthodoxy by pointing to Vatican II. This second point is undermined by the article itself, which describes the changes as a grassroots movement: "Religious have, in many ways, outdistanced the hierarchical Church in their practical commitment to the mission of being in, with, and for the world, and in accepting the implications of this commitment...."[18] Joseph Becker's history of the Jesuits paints a detailed picture of the many ways that the hierarchy was deceived, manipulated, and undermined by radical priests and seminarians.[19]

But the "naming-and-not-exactly-blaming" of Vatican II is undermined in the article in another important way. It launches into a specific critique of each of the three vows of chastity, obedience, and poverty. But nowhere in that critique is there any evidence of a Vatican II influence. The fingerprints of psychology, on the other hand, are everywhere. For the purpose of understanding the abuse scandal, it will be necessary to focus on the vow of chastity.

Celibacy

Once again, we read in the *New Catholic En-*

cyclopedia:

> "Chastity, or celibacy . . . has been explained theologically in many ways in the course of history. Most of these explanations are considered unsatisfactory today because they involve, explicitly or implicitly, a negative attitude toward sexuality and a denigration of marriage as a Christian vocation. The practice flowing from such theologies though admirable in many respects, is often seen today *as overly characterized by fear, guilt, and repression and as leading to serious affective underdevelopment in many religious.*"[20]

This is an explicitly Freudian critique—we are psychologically damaged by denying our sexual desires. The implications for homosexuality and a host of other sexual sins are obvious, as the "progressive majority" explains:

> "The contemporary realization of the importance of sexuality in human life . . . has led to a serious revision of both the theology and the practice of religious celibacy. This reflection has been influenced by the increasingly open discussion of sexuality in general, and particularly of homosexuality...."[21]

There in that brief statement is contained the whole of the sexual revolution and its impact on the Church: Sex is too important to be denied.

So what are we to make, then, of the vow of celibacy? The NCE says that it shouldn't be a permanent vow.[22] And what about the condemnation of homosexuality in the Bible? Clearly the Apostles did not have the "benefit" of modern psychology. And that meant that the belief in the infallibility of biblical teaching had to be mistaken. The laws of the Bible could not be God-given, for the Bible is just like any other fallible human pronouncement. Growing numbers in the Church were becoming convinced that traditional Christian morality needed to be revised in light of advances being made in science, most especially, in psychology.[23]

As Joseph Becker tells us in his history: "Humanistic psychology . . . included a judgment that the traditional religious lifestyle ran a serious danger of being a psychologically deprived life . . . ."[24] Becker tells the story of how a book —*Practice of Perfection and Christian Virtues*—had been the mandatory spiritual reading "for all Jesuit novices throughout the world."[25] Written in 1600 by the Spanish master of novices Alphonsus Rodriguez, the book became the target of criticism in the sixties because it "did not reflect the new findings" in psychology and because it "did not reflect modern scriptural exegesis *or modern sexual morality*."[26] Becker tells us: "In time, all the novitiates discontinued the practice of reading Rodriguez, and the typical modern novice has not so much as heard of the work."[27] What took its place according to Becker? Carl Rogers did.[28]

CLOSE ENCOUNTERS WITH CARL ROGERS

The biggest development in clinical therapy in the fifties was the shift away from mental illness. Previous to that, patients for therapy were exclusively of the neurotic kind—people who were suicidal or depressed or crippled by phobias. But the human potential movement was about helping *all* people achieve fulfillment through the development of their unique individuality. This meant that therapy was now for everybody, for there wasn't a soul around who couldn't use a little help in becoming all they could be. And California was the Mecca for the human potential movement.

It had the Esalen Institute in the North, situated along the beautiful Big Sur coast. And in the South were stationed the gurus of the movement—Abraham Maslow and Carl Rogers. And sandwiched right in between, we find the good sisters of the Immaculate Heart of Mary. Our story takes us to their convent.

Conscience—"The Authority Within"

They called it TFN—*Therapy For Normals*—and William Coulson, a collaborator with Rogers, described it as "non-directive self-exploration."[29] The purpose of this "non-directive therapy" was to put clients in touch with their consciences—"the authority within themselves," as Coulson described it in an interview.[30] Coulson elaborates on Rogers's therapeutic approach:

> He could disappear for people, and leave them in the presence of their consciences. You see, as a practicing Catholic layman, I thought that was pretty holy: that God was available to every person who had a decent upbringing, that he could self-consult, as it were, and hear God speaking to him. I was thinking of William James's idea that the conscience can provide access to the Holy Spirit.[31]

Coulson was put on a mission by Rogers to enlist the IHM sisters as participants in a study of Rogers's new group therapy. The "encounter" groups, as they were called, encouraged the partici-

Confronting the Pope of Suspicion

pants to share their personal feelings with the other group members. There were lots of hurt feelings as they shared how much they couldn't stand each other. Naturally, this created a lot of friction in the community, resulting in the formation of cliques and factions.[32]

But the nuns also opened up about tenderer feelings. And this led to friction of a whole different order. As the sisters talked about their desires and feelings of attraction, naturally the next step was to act on those feelings. Members of the therapy groups became sexually active with one another.[33] Some of the sisters became involved with their therapists. Others got involved with priests. Some became sexually active with each other. Coulson acknowledged in an interview that it had become commonplace at this time, and especially in California, for therapists to become sexually involved with their clients—a fact that shouldn't sit too well today in the wake of the #metoo movement.[34]

According to Coulson, he and Rogers did not approve of these developments, but they were powerless to stop the other therapists because it was built into Rogers's theory that people ought to bring out their unique feelings and desires. Maybe it wasn't in *them* to become sexually involved with their clients, but it was indeed in many of the practicing therapists at the time. Rogers had unleashed a "dictatorship of relativism" that he could not control:

> "Rogers didn't get people involved in sex games, but he couldn't prevent his followers from doing it, because all he could say was, 'Well, I don't do that.' Then his followers would say, 'Well, of course you don't do that, because you grew up in an earlier era; but we do, and it's marvelous: you have set us free to be ourselves and not carbon copies of you.'"[35]

Coulson stated in an interview that he and Rogers did not like what was happening in the IHM project, so they shut the study down a year early.[36] After only the first year, half of the nuns petitioned Rome to be released from their vows.[37] The order is effectively defunct in California.

❈ ❈ ❈

THE SEXUAL ABUSE OF MINORS

Rogers and Coulson worked their way up the California coast like modern day Junipero Serras. And they brought their missionary zeal with them to St. Anthony's Seminary in Santa Barbara. It is here that our story takes its darkest turn. This comes from *Sacrilege* by Dr. Leon Podles:

> Rogers and Coulson gave the same program at St. Anthony's Seminary. When the friars there looked into their inner selves and affirmed their deepest desires, a good proportion of them (about one-quarter) discovered that what they really wanted most of all was to have sex with fourteen-year-old boys, which they proceeded to do

for the next twenty years. The encounter groups had convinced them to believe that "when people do what they deeply want to do, it isn't immoral." The abuse had started before the encounter groups were formed, but after the encounter groups it vastly increased. After complaints of abuse surfaced, the Franciscans who ran St. Anthony's Seminary commissioned an inquiry. The board discovered that twenty-five percent, eleven out of the forty-four friars at the seminary had engaged in sex with the high school students there... [38]

One Master of Suspicion Repents

In an important but brief videotaped interview, Coulson describes how it was the intent of psychology to take over the Church. And at the end, he describes the horrible consequences of this tragic intervention. Speaking explicitly of the priest scandal, Coulson concluded:

"It's all because of the influence of psychology. Set aside the commandments was our advice, and get in touch with the feelings. Well, that's only good advice if we aren't sinners. But all of us are, as we have learned through our great distress."[39]

The Coulson Theory of Abuse

Coulson's mea culpa challenges the biggest myth about the scandal, namely that Church teaching on sexuality was to blame for it. On the contrary, it was the *abandonment* of that teaching that led to the scandal. Coulson clearly blames the humanistic psychology that he and Rogers aggressively promoted in the Catholic Church and that destroyed religious orders. It was a psychological theory that was blind to the darker side of human nature. Human beings were good and so were their desires. And sexuality was just too important to be denied. It was a new theory of human fulfillment and development that rejected Christian asceticism as psychologically harmful.

Rogers and Coulson worked with two-dozen religious groups, and by all accounts, they were successful missionaries. Celibacy was no longer taught or encouraged at a growing number of seminaries.[40] For as the *New Catholic Encyclopedia* stated, celibacy led to

"serious affective underdevelopment ... fear, guilt, and repression."[41]

Instead, sexual freedom was promoted. It was a psychological experiment that placed the individual's freedom and "conscience" above the moral law. And it rejected man's sinfulness as an artifact of religious superstition. An experiment that was supposed to liberate the individual and develop human potential ended in the sexual abuse of children instead. That is the professional opinion of perhaps the most qualified expert anywhere—one of the leading lights of the human potential movement.

The Sullins Report

A recent study by Dr. Paul Sullins of the Ruth Institute corroborates Coulson's theory of the sex abuse scandal. Sullins used data from a *Los Angeles Times* report that studied the growth of homosexual subcultures in seminaries. These were places where homosexuality was openly tolerated and even encouraged by the faculty and administration —obvious bastions of sexual liberation. He found that the spread of sexual liberation ideology in seminaries (as evidenced by the presence of homosexual subcultures) tracked very closely with the spread of sexual abuse, both of which peaked at the same time, in the late eighties through the early nineties.[42]

This is just more empirical evidence that sexual abuse was caused by the sexual revolution inside the Church. The scandal is linked *not to celibacy, but to the disappearance of celibacy* from religious life. This agreed with the findings of the second John Jay report. It wasn't *celibacy* in the seminaries that was linked to later sexual abuse. It was sexual activity during seminary and the use of pornography that showed a strong correlation to later sexual abuse.[43] If people understood what really caused the scandal, they wouldn't be leaving the Church. They'd be leaving the sexual revolution instead.

Pandora's Box Opened—From Relativism to Nihilism

Despite William Coulson's regrets and protestations, the impact of his work was irreversible. The human potential movement had set off a theological revolution inside the Church. And academic types got busy producing new theological texts that reflected the new thinking about sex. The NCE article on the vows serves as an excellent encapsulation of the new heretical orthodoxy inside the Church. In that brief article, we find the elevation of psychology over divine revelation. We find the consequent rejection of intrinsic evil in favor of a new freedom of conscience that respects individual differences—especially where sex is concerned. And we find the acceptance of homosexuality—the logical conclusion of these heresies. All that in just a brief article. To appreciate the full implications of these heresies, however, a more expansive treatment of the subject would be necessary. And the Catholic Theological Society of America was happy to oblige.

In 1977 the CTSA published *Human Sexuality: New Directions in American Catholic Thought* (HS). Here we find a comprehensive explication of these ideas: the elevation of subjective conscience and the rejection of intrinsic evil.[44] According to HS, sexual morality is always changing and only represents the arbitrary opinions of a particular society.[45] There is no objectively valid moral objection to *any sexual behavior.* The book mentions a few of our arbitrarily determined cultural prejudices — *incest and bestiality.*[46] The book's recommendation? "[E]nlightened and well integrated individuals might well free themselves of conflict by simply reflecting on the relativity of their society's sexual ethic and proceed discreetly with their own sexual project."[47] And with that, the descent into nihilism was complete.[48]

❋ ❋ ❋

THE JOHN PAUL REFORM

When John Paul acted quickly to condemn the book that permitted everything, *The New York Times* was quick to pounce.

> "There is a widespread conviction among Catholic officials that Pope John Paul II has decided to give high priority to the defense of conservative tenets of Catholic doctrine against liberal trends that have become increasingly visible within the clergy in the United States, Western Europe and Latin America."[49]

This was not a liberal/conservative issue, but a question of orthodoxy and decency. Was the defense of *bestiality* and *incest* really a plank in the reform platform of liberals? Not even conservatives held their liberal opponents in such low esteem as to accuse them of such abject depravity.

All throughout John Paul's pontificate, we see the highest attention paid to the theological crisis that had overtaken the Church. One of his earliest moves was to condemn *Human Sexuality.* But it wasn't his last—not by a long shot. The firing and punishment of various masters of suspicion occurred throughout his tenure: Charles Curran, Abp. Raymond Hunthausen, Edward Schillebeeckx, and Hans Küng. And there was the unprecedented take over of the Society of Jesus.[50]

And so many of his writings were addressed to this problem: *Veritatis Splendor, Familiaris Consortio, Fides Et Ratio, The Theology of the Body, The Catechism of the Catholic Church.* One of his most controversial efforts was *Ex Corde Ecclesiae*, which mandated that all theology departments be orthodox in their teaching. The "mandatum," as it was called, provoked an outcry of protest from academics who claimed that the intervention constituted an infringement of academic freedom.[51] And the bishops, always eager to avoid controversy and hard work, did not enforce it, so, today, the same heresies responsible for the sexual abuse crisis are protected under the banner of "academic freedom."

James Martin

Nowhere is the need for theological reform

Confronting the Pope of Suspicion

better embodied than in the person of Fr. James Martin. While his book *Building a Bridge* is more guarded, he openly campaigns for the normalization of homosexuality in his talks. He looks forward to the day when gay couples will be able to kiss at the sign of peace.[52] Now most Christians don't look forward to the committing of sin, so it is safe to conclude that Martin does not believe that homosexuality is sinful.

His stump speech includes a generous mash-up of spiritually accented bromides from humanistic psychology:

"God made you the way you are." "And you are beautifully and wonderfully made."[53]

We learn from Martin's book *Building a Bridge* (BB) that from premises such as these, homosexuals ought to inform their consciences.[54] And the conclusion that such an informed conscience should draw is that homosexuality is not intrinsically disordered, but merely "differently ordered."[55] And with that, Martin manages to square a theological circle—*a Catholic conscience can be properly formed and at variance with divine revelation and apostolic teaching.* Such a possibility is ruled out by Sacred Scripture (Gal. 1). It is ruled out by the Nicene Creed which upholds the apostolic foundations of the Church. And it is ruled out by *Veritatis Splendor* (VS).

In VS 56, John Paul the Great rules out the

possibility that personal conscience can ever be invoked as a justification for committing an intrinsic evil. What are some examples of intrinsic evil? The concept is from the Bible, John Paul tells us at VS 81, and he quotes from 1Cor. 6:9–10, which identifies some intrinsic evils:

> "Do you not know that the unrighteous will not inherit the kingdom of God? Do not be deceived; neither the immoral, nor idolaters, nor adulterers, nor sexual perverts, nor thieves, nor the greedy, nor drunkards, nor revilers, nor robbers will inherit the kingdom of God."

Because homosexuality is an intrinsic evil, an informed personal conscience can never approve of those acts. There are no exceptions or personal circumstances that can change that fact. This is the constant teaching of the Church going back to the Apostles. In short, although many people in the world may accept Martin's view of homosexuality, it is nevertheless incompatible with Catholic doctrine.

To put it bluntly, Martin's view of homosexuality is heretical. But whenever he is correctly identified as a heretic, Martin offers a most intriguing defense. He has the support of the bishops he tells us. Now anyone familiar with Church history should know that the support of the bishops is no evidence of orthodoxy, for plenty of bishops have been condemned for heresy. So the support that Martin enjoys from the bishops is hardly comforting; on the contrary, it is quite distressing evidence that a widespread heresy has reached to the highest levels of the Church. But it is the support from one bishop in particular that is of gravest concern—the bishop of Rome.

❈ ❈ ❈

POPE FRANCIS

Two years following the explosive Synod on the Family, Pope Francis gave James Martin a promotion, making him a consultant to the Vatican's communications office.[56] Martin's book *Building a Bridge* was about to be published and preparations were under way for the promotion of the World Meeting of Families in Ireland. The title of the conference was the "Joy of Love," and its purpose was to promote the ideas of *Amoris Laetitia* (Latin for *Joy of Love*). The published program for the conference included a photograph of a lesbian couple, and beside that photograph came the following *Amoris Laetitia*-inspired language:

> "While the Church upholds the ideal of marriage as a permanent commitment between a man and a woman, other unions exist which provide mutual support to the couple. Pope Francis encourages us never to exclude but to accompany these couples

Confronting the Pope of Suspicion

also, with love, care, and support."[57]

That a pro-LGBT message should be coming from an *Amoris Laetitia*-themed conference seemed to confirm the darkest suspicions about AL and the Synod that produced it—specifically, that a primary objective of that Synod was a reversal of doctrine on homosexuality.[58] The argument that the homosexual activism came from a hijacking of the conference by outsiders was not a credible explanation. For the World Meeting of Families was headed by Cdl. Kevin Farrell, a Vatican official and appointee of Pope Francis. Circumstantial evidence appeared to link Pope Francis to the pro-homosexual agenda in the Church. But if this is true, shouldn't we be able to locate such support in the pope's writings?

A prime piece of evidence comes from the preliminary document of the Synod on the Family that produced AL. The *Relatio* (*post disceptationem*) as it is called in Latin, (otherwise known as the interim report) contained a small section with the subheading "Welcoming Homosexual Persons." Here's what it said:

> Are our communities capable of... accepting and valuing their sexual orientation, without compromising Catholic doctrine on the family and matrimony? 51. The question of homosexuality leads to a serious reflection on how to elaborate real-

istic paths of affective growth and human and evangelical maturity integrating the sexual dimension: it appears therefore as an important educative challenge.[59]

When the Relatio was published, it was released to the news media before the Synod Fathers had a chance to look at it. Edward Pentin does an outstanding job of describing the bishops' reactions when they finally got a chance to read the document. Their verdict on the report was uniform. Those statements on homosexuality had never been discussed. So where did the *Relatio* come from? Clearly it came from those who were in charge of the Synod. And who put them in charge? Francis did. The only logical conclusion was obvious. Francis and his circle of allies were using the Synod to introduce doctrinal change on the subject of homosexuality.[60]

❊ ❊ ❊

AMORIS LAETITIA

The Language Problem

The explicitly pro-homosexual language of the *Relatio* never made it into the final document of *Amoris Laetitia*. And that was certainly due to the fury of the orthodox bishops who wouldn't stand for it. Nevertheless, the language of AL had problems of its own. Consider par. 303:

> "Recognizing the influence of such concrete factors, we can add that individual conscience needs to be better incorporated into the Church's praxis in certain situations which do not objectively embody our understanding of marriage. Naturally, every effort should be made to encourage the development of an enlightened conscience, formed and guided by

the responsible and serious discernment of one's pastor, and to encourage an ever greater trust in God's grace."

Situations that do not embody our understanding of marriage—clearly the reference here is to the divorced and remarried, since AL directly addresses that issue (par. 297, etc.). In par. 293, Francis discusses cohabiting couples. Certainly those relationships also do not "embody our understanding of marriage." But given that the World Meeting of Families deliberately included same-sex couples, and given the *Relatio* that preceded AL, there could be no doubt that this passage referred to same-sex couples as well.

Francis is referring to non-marital relationships to be sure. But there are an infinite number of non-marital relationships, and it's a safe bet that he intended a narrower category. The parent-child relationship, for example, is non-marital, but that's certainly not what Francis is thinking about in par. 303. The same would be true for the pet-to-owner relationship—employer to employee, grandparent to grandchild, king to subjects, teacher to student, car owner to car, hamburger to hamburger-eater... It's safe to say that none of these relationships are what par. 303 had in mind. What Francis is driving at here is a category of non-marital relationship that nevertheless shares in some of the attributes of marriage. Can you guess what that mysterious attribute might be? Sex. Francis is talking about sex-

Confronting the Pope of Suspicion

ual relationships *outside* of marriage.

And so the proper question to ask about AL 303 is this: Why should the role of individual conscience be so important in cases where the rules are so clear, as John Paul reminded us in *Veritatis Splendor* 81? Adultery, fornication, and homosexuality are intrinsically evil, and no special circumstances can change that fact. The discernment of special factors or situations is actually *irrelevant* in these cases. AL 303 is calling for a situational ethics to be applied in cases where such an ethics is expressly forbidden by apostolic doctrine, as John Paul the Great reminded us in *Veritatis Splendor*.

AL 303 and other passages like it caused so much consternation that a group of Cardinals submitted official questions to the pope for clarification. Here is one of those questions, also known as *dubia*. It pertains to the passage above:

"After *Amoris Laetitia* (303) does one still need to regard as valid the teaching of St. John Paul II's *encyclical Veritatis Splendor, 56, based on sacred Scripture and on the Tradition of the Church, that excludes a creative interpretation of the role of conscience and that emphasizes that conscience can never be authorized to legitimate exceptions to absolute moral norms that prohibit intrinsically evil acts by virtue of their object?*"[61]

Pope Francis never answered the dubia, but

we can figure out the answers for ourselves with a good degree of certainty. Consider paragraph 300 from AL:

"300. If we consider the immense variety of concrete situations such as those I have mentioned, it is understandable that neither the Synod nor this Exhortation could be expected to provide a <u>new set of general rules</u>, canonical in nature and applicable to all cases. What is possible is simply a renewed encouragement to undertake a responsible personal and pastoral discernment of particular cases..."

Does Francis mean to imply that AL invalidates the *old* set of general rules? Why then the "expectation" for a *new* set of rules? The old set are just fine, thank you very much. They are called the Ten Commandments and they aren't going away — which is why they were written in stone *by God Himself* in the first place. Let us also be clear that Francis, here, is confessing difficulty in a task that posed no problem for John Paul the Great—in the enumeration of general rules that apply in all cases. They include the intrinsic evils, which are found in the Bible. But Francis knows all of this. Thus, the only conclusion that can be drawn is that, in paragraph 300 of *Amoris Laetita,* Francis has rejected the concept of intrinsic evil. [62] He is denying what St. Paul wrote and taught and the Church has constantly taught until the publication of *Amoris Laetitia*, namely, that there are rules and standards of moral conduct that apply in all cases regardless of

Confronting the Pope of Suspicion

the particular circumstances. And to violate these rules is to forfeit salvation.

Thus, when Francis says in par. 300, above, that all that is possible is "a discernment of particular cases," he is stating a falsehood. He left out the most important and essential possibility of all, which is this: It is the duty to proclaim the Church's magisterial teaching concerning sex outside of marriage. It is the duty to teach that sex outside of marriage is always and everywhere wrong.[63]

Plagiarism in Amoris Laetitia?[64]

Another major issue with the language of *Amoris Laetitia* concerns its remarkable similarity to previously published works. Consider the most famous line from *Amoris Laetitia*, par. 37:

"We have been called to form consciences, not to replace them."

Compare that line to this one from *Human Sexuality* —the book condemned by Pope John Paul:

"[G]uidelines will serve to enlighten the judgment of conscience; they cannot replace it."[65]

Did Pope Francis, or his ghostwriters, borrow the line from *Human Sexuality*? No attribution is given for the snappiest line in AL. If in fact the line was plagiarized from *Human Sexuality*, it is understandable why the writer did not credit the source. After all, the book had been condemned, not once, but

49

twice by the Vatican.[66] The book explicitly rejects the concept of intrinsic evil. In fact, it is so zealous to deny this bedrock principle of Judeo-Christian morals that the book wouldn't even categorically condemn bestiality or incest.

Francis and the *Humanae Vitae* Connection

Nevertheless it is possible that the line was not stolen from *Human Sexuality*. It may have been stolen from the *Medico-Moral Guide* instead. *Human Sexuality* cites *Medico-Moral* as the original source for the quote. That's the document from the Catholic Health Association of Canada that instituted the Canadian bishops' original guidelines[67] for the implementation of *Humanae Vitae* (HV) at Catholic hospitals. What was that policy? It said that HV's teaching was only a guideline that could be overridden by one's personal conscience. According to Msgr. Vincent Foy, this was an endorsement by the Canadian bishops of Charles Curran's views on personal conscience. And it led to the loss of Catholic identity in Canadian hospitals. They were soon giving out as much artificial contraception as the secular hospitals.[68]

Is *Medico-Moral* the unnamed source in *Amoris Laetitia*? The implications are huge if it is. It may provide an interpretive lens for comprehending the role played by conscience in Francis' moral theology. Which should make a lot of people uneasy. If Francis is endorsing the view of conscience

Confronting the Pope of Suspicion

in *Medico-Moral*, then he is essentially agreeing with Charles Curran's view of conscience—the view condemned by John Paul the Great in *Veritatis Splendor*. It is the view that got Curran kicked out of Catholic University of America—the very same view of conscience that led the Vatican to strip Curran of his credentials to teach Catholic theology.[69] Thus, the rhetorical question is no longer rhetorical—*Is the pope Catholic?*

Is Pope Francis promoting a view of personal conscience and situational ethics that is incompatible with the Church's doctrine of intrinsic evil? He seemed to acknowledge as much in his comments to the Society of Jesus at their General Congregation 36 in Rome. When he was asked a question about his own morality of discernment, he contrasted it with what the Church previously taught when he was in seminary—an older, traditional morality that was "rigid." Here are Francis' exact words taken from a report by Pete Baklinski at *Life Site News*:

> "Discernment is the key element: the capacity for discernment. I note the absence of discernment in the formation of priests. We run the risk of getting used to 'white or black,' to that which is legal. We are rather closed, in general, to discernment. One thing is clear: today, in a certain number of seminaries, a rigidity that is far from a discernment of situations has been introduced. And that is dangerous, because it

can lead us to a conception of morality that has a casuistic sense." [70]

What Francis is describing above is the same situational ethics that we see throughout AL: individuals enjoy the freedom to exercise their personal consciences to discern from particular situations a moral course of action.[71] There is nothing anti-Catholic about that, provided that the domain of intrinsic evils is respected. Indeed, many moral decisions are properly discerned by an assessment of particular situations and circumstances. Is it moral to take a person's life? That depends on the circumstances. If a person is trying to kill you, then you are permitted to do what is necessary to defend your life and other innocent lives. Certainly the Church has never denied that situational ethics has a legitimate place in authentic moral reasoning.

But Francis contrasts this morality of discernment that he favors with an older moral theology that he calls a "decadent scholasticism" that is too "black and white" and overly rigid.[72] This was the moral theology that educated his generation, he tells us, and is still being taught in too many seminaries.[73] Could he be referring to the doctrine of intrinsic evil? The very doctrine defended by John Paul the Great in *Veritatis Splendor*? What else could he be referring to?[74] Thus, the question that must be answered by anyone with an interest in preserving the integrity of Catholic doctrine is this. How can we reconcile the situational

Confronting the Pope of Suspicion

ethics favored by Pope Francis with the doctrine of intrinsic evil of Church Tradition, if even Francis himself characterizes them as incompatible?

And AL 303 pinpoints that incompatibility: Francis is denying that the Christian prohibition against sex outside of marriage is absolute. Recall that par. 303 calls for the application of situational ethics to relationships "which do not objectively embody our understanding of marriage." This would include the divorced and remarried. But it could include same-sex relationships and co-habiting couples as well, as we have already observed.

Whether Francis is willing to admit it, he belongs to the school that believes that the church got sexuality wrong. Francis' praise of Bernard Häring certainly supports this interpretation.[75] Häring was an early outspoken critic of *Humanae Vitae* who argued, like Charles Curran and so many others, that a person could disregard the teachings of HV in good conscience.[76] In Häring's criticism of *Veritatis Splendor*, he called into question John Paul's understanding of sexuality:

> "Let us ask our pope: Are you sure your confidence in your supreme human, professional and religious competence in matters of moral theology and particularly sexual ethics is truly justified?"[77]

Häring's ideas were heavily influenced by the humanistic psychology of Maslow and

Rogers.[78] And this explains his criticism of Church teaching on sexuality. He accepted the psychological critique of the masters of suspicion, which rejected a theological understanding of human nature. In place of the absolute moral norms of the Church, Häring advocated instead for a morality of discernment that took into account the many concrete factors of a situation, including psychological factors that considered subjective elements like desires and feelings to be important. What constituted a correct moral judgment for one person might be quite different for some other person with different psychological and sexual "needs."[79] Thus, it was up to the individual to use his conscience in order to discern the correct moral course of action in a given situation.[80]

And so the circle is completed. The elevation of conscience we see in the work of Carl Rogers and William Coulson is the very same as the one we find in AL—courtesy of Bernard Häring. And it is the very same elevation of conscience that Coulson eventually admitted was directly responsible for sexual abuse in the Church:

> *"It's all because of the influence of psychology. Set aside the commandments was our advice, and get in touch with the feelings. Well, that's only good advice if we aren't sinners. But all of us are, as we have learned through our great distress."*[81]

One of the chief masters of suspicion realized what his psychological theories had done to the Church, and he repented of his Pelagian heresies. Can the pope of suspicion do the same?

Amoris Laetitia Makes No Doctrinal Changes?

The defenders of Pope Francis and AL insist that doctrine is left untouched and only pastoral recommendations are made. This is not true. We have already seen that paragraphs 300 and 304 deny that there are general rules that apply without exception. This is a rejection of the doctrine of intrinsic evil that is upheld by John Paul as an apostolic and therefore essential teaching. Even so, it is possible to evaluate *Amoris Laetitia* in the manner favored by its defenders. So, let us set aside for a moment the question of doctrinal fidelity and focus instead on its pastoral recommendations.

The Francis Paradigm of Conscience Formation: The Priest as Sex Therapist

Does Amoris Laetitia make good pastoral recommendations for conscience formation and moral decision-making? We are referred to a process of discernment with a local pastor where all the important factors can be weighed, including psychological factors. Here is par. 303 again:

> "Recognizing the influence of such concrete factors, we can add that individ-

ual conscience needs to be better incorporated into the Church's praxis in certain situations which do not objectively embody our understanding of marriage. Naturally, every effort should be made to encourage the development of an enlightened conscience, formed and guided by the responsible and serious discernment of one's pastor, and to encourage an ever greater trust in God's grace."

In the Francis paradigm, people in irregular sexual situations need a priest to accompany them to help them work out their complex situations. Exactly what the priest will say or do is not clear or what his guide will be. The Church's Magisterium fulfilled this essential teaching role in *Veritatis Splendor* (64), but in *Amoris Laetitia*, we are told that the Magisterium is not always necessary (par.3). Nor will the priest have absolute moral norms to guide him because paragraph 300 tells us that such rules are not possible. "What *is* possible" is the "thinking of pastors and theologians" that will help us to get clarity on these issues (par. 2, par. 300). Does that sound like good pastoral advice?

What if James Martin is your pastor? His statements in various places are well summarized by this *Washington Post* article from Sr. Jeannine Gramick:

"Catholic thinking dictates that we should

Confronting the Pope of Suspicion

use the evidence we find in the natural world to help us reach our conclusions. *Many Catholics have reflected on the scientific evidence that homosexuality is a natural variant in human sexuality, and understand that lesbian and gay love is as natural as heterosexual love."*[82]

The pope's support of James Martin is disturbing because it is clear from Martin's writing and lectures that he believes an informed conscience can justify homosexuality. But such a conscience is clearly not being informed by Scripture or Tradition because these condemn homosexuality as an intrinsic evil. Martin has come out and said that the Bible is wrong about homosexuality.[83] It should be obvious that under the new Francis paradigm, James Martin is free to tell young Catholics that it is okay to be gay because the Bible is wrong about a lot of things. What are the guidelines in AL to rein in a maverick like Martin? There are none. In fact, the indiscriminate use of psychology in AL actually encourages arguments like Martin's because so many psychological theories today openly advocate for the normalization of homosexuality.

Or what if your pastor was The Most Reverend Bishop Anthony O'Connell? Podles tells us that when O'Connell was a seminary rector, one of the seminarians, Christopher Dixon, came to him for counseling. Years earlier, Dixon had been molested by a parish priest when he was an altar boy, and he still suffered from the trauma. So he came to O'Connell for help. What sort of accompaniment did His Excellency offer? According to Dixon, O'Connell asked him to disrobe, whereupon O'Connell promptly accompanied the troubled young man to the bedroom. O'Connell later explained his behavior: "'What I was trying to do was work with a youngster who has personal issues. We're talking about the late 70s. In Catholic theology there were different kinds of approaches.'" [84] O'Connell claimed that his technique came from Masters and Johnson.[85]

Or you might get Fr. Rudy Kos as your spiritual director. Podles tells us that a boy with homosexual inclinations had been referred to Kos for counseling. What was Kos's approach? He explained that the Bible didn't really condemn homosexuality. Then he molested the boy.[86] And whenever Paul Shanley had boys referred to him for counseling, they would receive a course in "situation ethics" before he sodomized them.[87]

The Link to Homosexuality

These are but a few examples that illustrate a clear pattern in much of the sexual abuse that took place in the Church. With so many of the male victims being teenagers, it makes sense to realize that the abuse was not carried out by physical force, but by persuasion. Priests exploited their role as teacher and counselor to preach to underage minors that homosexuality was morally permissible. Two factors greatly facilitated the seduction process. First was the promotion of psychological theories that encouraged sexual permissiveness. Second was the rejection of the Christian morality that condemned that sexual permissiveness as intrinsically evil.

The Failure of *Amoris Laetitia*

Tragically this is the error of *Amoris Laetitia*. AL continues the errors of the new theology by denying that there are general rules of sexual behavior that are absolute. Is that good pastoral advice for priests who have the burden to counsel Catholics on matters of sexual ethics? It was precisely the rejection of objective and absolute moral norms that created the sexual abuse scandal. Homosexuality, fornication, and adultery are all intrinsically evil. Pedophilia and ephebophilia are intrinsically evil. The theology textbooks that formed our priests like Andre Guindon's *The Sexual Language* had trouble remembering these things.[88] Had *Amoris Laetitia* clearly defended the teaching that sex outside of marriage is intrinsically evil, it could have served as a practical corrective to the terrible theological errors of the twentieth century. Instead it spreads those errors—the very errors that led to a demonic epidemic of sexual abuse.

Thus, when we analyze AL on the merits of its praxis—as its defenders would have us do—what we find is that it has no merits. *Amoris Laetitia* continues the very same pastoral errors that caused an epidemic of clergy sexual abuse in the seventies, eighties, and nineties.

Hermeneutic of Continuity?

We can identify several concepts contained in *Amoris Laetitia* that are traceable to the dissenting theology of the late twentieth century:

1. *Universal Inclusion* In chapter eight of AL, with regard to those who do not follow the Church's teachings on sexual morality, Francis tells us that "the logic of integration is the key to their pastoral care" (par. 299). He even goes so far as to suggest that those in mortal sin may be admitted to communion (par. 305, note 351). This was the position of the NCE, which also called for universal participation.[89] You will recall that the NCE article declared that the "progressive majority" approved of homosexual practice for priests. Nowhere did it imply that these priests were unworthy of communion. What it openly declared instead was that the "progressive majority" no longer followed the rules. So why take the communion rule so seriously? Universal inclusion is also promoted in *Human Sexuality*. It says that homosexuals have a right to full participation in the sacraments, including the Eucharist.[90]

Confessors who disagree need to keep their uninformed and "unproven" opinions to themselves.[91]

2. *Cultural Relativism (AL 3)* According to *Human Sexuality*, traditional Christian morality is not a divinely revealed universal law but merely the expression of the particular likes and dislikes of a particular culture.[92] Christian morality is just one set of arbitrary rules with no more validity than the rules expressed by different cultures. One should feel free, therefore, to ignore the sexual morality of Christianity and adopt the values of a different culture.[93] What do some of these other cultural values include? It's quite a list: fornication, homosexuality, mate-swapping, incest, bestiality. . . . Does AL go as far as HS does in its application of cultural relativism? No it does not. But what the cultural relativism of both AL and HS share in common is the denial of any possibility of a universal moral law, a clear contradiction of Scripture and Sacred Tradition. In fact, this was the very purpose of introducing cultural relativism at AL 3: Francis is including "cultural differences" in his very long list of factors that can render a general moral principle invalid.

3. *Conscience Formation*. On the question of proper conscience formation, here again,

we see that AL shares more in common with the theology of dissent than with *Veritatis Splendor*. VS is clear that there are teachings on sexual morality that are exceptionless. If AL is in continuity with this traditional teaching—a teaching that goes back to the Apostles themselves, and indeed to Moses—it certainly is not clear. Nowhere does AL defend the concept of intrinsic evils or the concept of exceptionless moral rules more generally. On the contrary, it quite explicitly rejects that idea in multiple places, as we have already established.[94] In place of the Church's traditional morality, we are given a morality of discernment that must take into account psychological factors and cultural differences and a host of other situations and circumstances to help us make a correct moral decision. How do these situations and circumstances balance with the Church's teaching on intrinsic evil? AL is quite clear that it is the particular situations that are decisive on questions of sexual morality. The Church's teaching on intrinsic evil does not apply to sexual ethics, regardless of what the Apostles may have taught.

Regarding the role of the Magisterium, *Veritatis Splendor* 64 repeats the teaching of Vatican II that it is essential to conscience formation. AL 3 explicitly denies this.

4. *The Presentation of Moral Norms as Ideals (AL 307)* The NCE article does the same with religious vows. In the latter, it is clear that the presentation of vows as ideals means that, for some individuals with a particular psychological constitution, the religious vows are not mandatory. So, for some priests and religious, if the denial of sex would be detrimental to their "total affective and psychosexual well-being," then those individuals would not be under any obligation to abide by their vows.[95] Nor are they required to conform to biblical morality if they are gay. Does AL intend the same by presenting traditional moral obligations as ideals? It isn't clear. What is clear is that AL agrees that psychological factors need to be considered in the discernment of one's moral obligations. Which leads to the next disturbing feature of *Amoris Laetitia*.

5. *The Role of Psychology* (AL 302) The carte blanche granted to psychology in AL is problematic. Nowhere in AL can you find any criticism of psychological theory. This is a problem because many of the new ideas of psychology directly contradicted the Church's teachings on sexuality. And the theological revolutionaries of the

seventies knew it and did not deny it. In fact, they openly proclaimed it. (Read Guindon's introduction to *The Sexual Language* sometime.) Thus, when AL explicitly recommends the use of psychology for moral discernment without indicating that some psychological theories are incompatible with Church teaching, it has smuggled *doctrinal* error into the Church. Homosexuality is intrinsically disordered regardless of what Masters and Johnson think about it. Regardless of what James Martin and Sr. Jeannine Gramick and the "St. Gallen Mafia"[96] think about it. End of story. And the same is true for masturbation, fornication, the viewing of pornography, and any sexual activity outside of marriage: psychological theories that approve these activities as healthy and natural expressions of sexuality are incompatible with Church doctrine and are not acceptable for moral discernment and authentic conscience formation. The absence of any such clear statement in *Amoris Laetitia* is evidence of the document's bad faith.

There can be no doubt that *Amoris Laetitia* shares much in common with the theology of dissent—a theology of situational ethics that was condemned by John Paul the Great in *Veritatis Splen-*

dor. Does that mean that *Amoris Laetitia* must also be condemned? That depends. If it was simply Francis' intention to publish a document that endorsed and promoted this theology, then AL must be condemned. *Lumen Gentium* 25 is clear that not even a pope can change the settled teachings of the Magisterium, and the Church's teaching on sex outside of marriage has been settled doctrine since the very beginning.[97]

On the other hand, perhaps Francis intended something more innovative. Rather than merely rubber stamp the theology of dissent, perhaps *Amoris Laetitia's* real project was to effect a grand synthesis of orthodox and dissenting doctrine on the question of sexual morality. If this is the real intent of AL, it is stated nowhere in the document. For anyone who claims such a thesis, the burden is clearly on them to prove it. And it is difficult to imagine what such a synthesis would even look like. The Church teaches that sex outside the boundaries of monogamous marriage and procreation is always wrong without exception. The dissenters deny this. What reconciliation can there be between such diametrically opposite positions? What synthesis could be achieved that would not violate the law of non-contradiction a thousand ways to Sunday?[98]

John Gravino

* * *

CAN WE REFORM THE POPE OF SUSPICION?

Thus, there is just no way to deny the tragic fact. In *Amoris Laetitia,* our present pope has weighed in on the most controversial theological dispute of the twentieth century, and he took the side of the dissenters against Sacred Scripture, against the Doctors and Fathers of the Church—against God's own Ten Commandments.[99]

The only possible defense for such a doctrinal train-wreck is the one proclaimed the loudest by Francis partisans, namely, that AL proposes no doctrinal changes, only changes in pastoral practice.[100] But, as was already pointed out, its pastoral recommendations are a disaster as well. The recommendation that priests be trained as sex therapists who ignore the exceptionless rule that sex outside of marriage is intrinsically evil—this was the pastoral approach that led to an epidemic of sexual abuse.

In the obscure history of twentieth century theology, we discover the causes of sexual abuse in the Church. And we discover as well, the theological influences that shaped Pope Francis and the ideas in AL. Francis was in Jesuit seminary in the sixties when these ideas were beginning to appear in Catholic seminaries. So it should be no surprise that they influenced Francis' own theological formation. Reading AL indicates that Francis was entirely persuaded by the psychological critique of the masters of suspicion, making him, in effect, the first pope of suspicion. Like the masters of suspicion and the theology of dissent that they inspired, AL rejects the application of exceptionless rules in matters of sexual ethics. In so doing, it rejects the concept of intrinsic evil and is therefore guilty of the same errors that created the sexual abuse crisis.

While most global crises are difficult to analyze because they are attributable to a massive tangle of causes and coincidences, the sexual abuse scandal in the Church is quite simple. Dr. Sullins's research confirms that when orthodox teaching was firmly in place in our seminaries and theology departments, there was no sexual abuse crisis.[101] It was the introduction of relativism and situational ethics that created an atmosphere of

Confronting the Pope of Suspicion

sexual permissiveness. And it was this permissiveness that ignited the conflagration of sexual abuse in the Church. Thus for any reform to be effective, it must reject this sexual permissiveness and return to the Gospel teaching. The traditional and apostolic teaching that sex outside of marriage is intrinsically evil must always be defended. No contrary view or theory coming from psychology or any other branch of science is ever admissible. The Church cannot admit any theory—psychological, scientific, or otherwise—that contradicts the apostolic doctrines of our faith.

Inquisition Redux

Now the modernists both inside and outside the Church will greet such a declaration with raucous derision and revilement. "The Church is anti-science!" they will declare. They will recount the story of Galileo ad nauseam. The people of faith need to take notice of these arguments and not be so quick to dismiss them. This is a serious objection to our faith, and it deserves a serious answer. John Paul the Great gave these objections a serious answer in many places—certainly in *Fides et Ratio* and *The Theology of the Body*: the Church's faith is no obstacle to scientific progress.

Ultimately, the Church does not defend its teachings because they are old, or in the Bible, or because the Apostles wrote them down, or even because "Jesus said so." The Church defends Her teachings because She believes they are true. If any teaching could be *proven* false, then not even the fact that Jesus taught it would be justification for continuing to believe something that had been proven false. The proper response to those who would accuse Christians of a "decadent scholasticism" because they continue to believe the perennial teachings of Christianity is to point out that those who were so quick to abandon the faith did so prematurely. Psychology never proved its case against Christianity—quite the contrary in fact.

Predictions Confirmed; Psychology Overturned

Today we can plainly see that the sexual liberation movement did not live up to its advanced billing. It did not succeed in making us better human beings as it promised. Instead of self-actualization, we got self-destruction. Instead of supermen, we got sex addicts and child molesters.[102] One of the chief architects of the humanistic psychology movement, William Coulson would come to admit that humanistic psychology was a terrible failure and that it was directly responsible for the sexual abuse scandal in the Church.[103] And at the same time that sexual abuse was peaking in the Church, and people everywhere were living the gospel according to Carl Rogers, violent crime in America was soaring to unprecedented levels in every category tracked by the FBI.[104]

Thus, what the evidence from the Me gen-

Confronting the Pope of Suspicion

eration taught us was that humanistic psychology was wrong to praise the instinctual passions as a vehicle for human health and happiness. The astronomically high rates of violent crime and sexual abuse associated with the "I'm okay, you're okay" generation confirmed exactly what the Church has always taught about the passions—that they are rightly called deadly sins and that it is far better to deny them than to follow them (1Pt. 2:11). This scientific vindication of the Bible certainly would have come as no surprise to John Paul the Great. He predicted it.[105]

Although humanistic psychology failed to deliver on its promise to help people achieve their potential, it did, nevertheless, succeed in confirming a few Bible predictions—like this one from the prophet Malachi for instance:

> "And now, O priests, this command is for you. If you will not listen, if you will not lay it to heart to give glory to my name, says the LORD of hosts, then I will send the curse upon you and I will curse your blessings; indeed I have already cursed them, because you do not lay it to heart. Behold, I will rebuke your offspring, and spread dung upon your faces, the dung of your offerings, and I will put you out of my presence. So shall you know that I have sent this command to you, that my covenant with Levi may hold, says the LORD of

hosts. My covenant with him was a covenant of life and peace, and I gave them to him, that he might fear; and he feared me, he stood in awe of my name. True instruction was in his mouth, and no wrong was found on his lips. He walked with me in peace and uprightness, and he turned many from iniquity. For the lips of a priest should guard knowledge, and men should seek instruction from his mouth, for he is the messenger of the LORD of hosts. But you have turned aside from the way; you have caused many to stumble by your instruction; you have corrupted the covenant of Levi, says the LORD of hosts, and so I make you despised and abased before all the people, inasmuch as you have not kept my ways but have shown partiality in your instruction" (Mal. 2: 1–9).

Confronting the Pope of Suspicion

It is now dawning on growing numbers of people that the sexual abuse scandal constitutes the gravest Church crisis in centuries. The solution, however, is simple, even if it proves difficult to implement. It follows the blueprint provided to us by Pope St. John Paul the Great in *Veritatis Splendor* and *Ex Corde Ecclesiae*. It is this: To proclaim the splendor of truth and enforce it. The priest scandal serves as a powerful reminder of this truth—that men become monsters when they abandon the Word of

Confronting the Pope of Suspicion

God. And that Word includes the divine teaching on sexual morality, which no man has the authority to subvert. Indeed, there are laws that are absolute, and to willfully disobey them is to forfeit salvation.

Is it too much to hope that the clergy will return to orthodoxy? Keep in mind that every bishop today was a seminarian during the tumultuous era of sexual liberation, and it has become increasingly evident during the Francis era that quite a few of them are followers of this progressive theology. Thus, more and more, it will be up to the laity—armed with a *newer* evangelization—to set things right in the Church. Already, there are positive signs in this direction, including the Red Hat Report sponsored by Better Church Governance.[106] We need to see more efforts like this. Above all, we must pray for and materially support our faithful priests and bishops.

And what is to be done about Pope Francis? There is disagreement about whether there exists enough evidence to remove the pope for heresy. Although it was not the purpose of this tract to make such an argument, nevertheless, the evidence presented here should help to make the case for heresy stronger. As previously stated above, *Amoris Laetitia* is nothing more than a recapitulation of the theology of dissent. Thus, the ideas in AL have already been condemned by a competent authority—by John Paul the Great himself in *Veritatis Splendor*.[107]

Regrettably, the Church is a very long way from recovery, and it is difficult, indeed, to find any light in our present dark valley. May the Lord be our Light. And may He shepherd us to greener pasture. Amen.

❋ ❋ ❋

POSTSCRIPT 2021:

Amoris Laetitia—Trojan Horse for Gay Fascism

Since Pope Francis declared 2021 to be a "Year of Reflection on *Amoris Laetitia*," I have decided to cooperate in this "reflection" project by releasing *Confronting the Pope of Suspicion* (CPS) in this new, expanded paperback edition you have before you. And I have added this postscript in order to comment on the important events that have transpired since CPS was published in the spring of 2019. My first comment pertains to this year of "reflection." It is nothing of the sort. Pope Francis isn't calling for a year of objective analysis of his book. He is calling for a year of promotion and praise for *Amoris Laetitia*. He is calling for a year of *implementation.* What a disaster for the Church and for souls.

This year of "reflection" kicks off on March 19th, so expect to find programs and retreats dedicated to praising the worst papal publication in the history of the Church. And that's not hyperbole. As I stated in my book *Confronting the Pope of Suspicion*: "Francis and his circle of allies were . . . introduc[ing] doctrinal change on the subject of homosexuality."[108]

The "December Massacre"

That headline was too hot to print when my book was first published in May of 2019.[109] But just seven months later, in December, this "controversial" claim was vindicated in spades. I've called it the "December Massacre." First, the German bishops announced the convening of a synod to reevaluate the Church's teaching on sexual morality from a more "scientific" perspective.[110] And what this new "scientific" perspective presumably demonstrated is that *homosexuality is a natural expression of human sexuality*—a direct assault on the Gospel and two-thousand years of teaching.[111] What was the justification for such a dramatic reversal of Scriptural teaching according to the German bishops? *Amoris Laetitia*.[112] Did the Vatican issue a response? In a manner of speaking. They agreed with the Germans. Only days after the German press release, the Vatican announced the publication of a new book that argued that the Bible was not qualified to teach on certain contemporary moral issues.[113] What was one of those issues? Homosexuality. According to excerpts of the Vatican text, we need "*science*" to help us understand today's moral controversies. Understand how radical this is. Within days of each other, the German bishops and the Vatican issued separate statements which agree on the same heretical proposition, namely, that the Bible—the Word of God—no longer has the authority to give us moral commandments, especially in the area of sexuality, and, more specifically, *homosexuality*. Did the pope have anything to say? Yes he did. In his Christmas address to the Curia—which also took place in December, 2019—he said that the Church was two-hundred years behind the times and that the Church needed—guess what— to catch up? "SCIENCE."[114]

Complete Vindication for *Confronting the Pope of Suspicion*

Despite all the praises and excuses made for *Amoris Laetitia* by professional Catholics in the media who should have known better, my book's critique of Amoris was completely vindicated by the December Massacre.[115] In CPS, I showed how *Amoris Laetitia* elevated science while denigrating Scripture and Tradition, just as the Germans are doing today. And, just as I argued in CPS, the German bishops have now publicly confirmed that, in fact, Amoris was a green light from the pontiff to mainstream the heretical ideas that were secretly being taught in seminary, specifically, the heresy that "science" should replace the Bible as the authority for understanding sexual morality. And completely disregarding the warnings of the dubia cardinals that the ideas in Amoris were explicitly condemned by Pope John Paul II in *Veritatis Splendor*, the clergy came out in force to promote *Amoris Laetitia* anyway. It wasn't just the German bishops who were guilty of this terrible heresy.

Confronting the Mass Apostasy in the Church

The December Massacre refutes the naïve theory, bandied about in some prominent journals, that the Germans were acting unilaterally.[116] My book showed that these heresies were not unique to the Germans at all. They were decades old and international in scope. The entire Jesuit order worldwide was infected by them. In the United States, these ideas were aggressively promoted through such institutions as the Catholic Theological Society of America and the Catholic University of America. Today, the German bishops themselves argue that their heretical ideas come from *Amoris Laetitia*. My book showed that the German bishops are right about that. And today, the American Jesuit Fr. James Martin has been quite active promoting the very same message. Thus the conclusion is painful but obvious. This most certainly is not just some crazy German thing as some influential people have tried to characterize it. It's is a global heresy inside the Church aptly summed up for us by another American, Sr. Jeannine Gramick of the pro-LGBT organization New Ways Ministry. Here's what she wrote in the *Washington Post* before *Amoris Laetitia* was ever written:

> Catholic thinking dictates that we should use the evidence we find in the natural world to help us reach our conclusions. Many Catholics have reflected on the scientific evidence that homosexuality is a natural variant in human sexuality, and understand that lesbian and gay love is as natural as heterosexual love.[117]

As I warned in *Confronting the Pope of Suspicion* (CPS), the heresy is so old now that its ideas were being taught when the present generation of bishops and cardinals were in seminary. Pope Francis himself, now in his eighties, was ordained in 1969 when these heresies were already in full swing. So we should not be surprised to discover that a great number of priests actually support the Amoris heresy. We should not be confused or incredulous when someone like Fr. James Martin can honestly state that he has the support of many bishops. If you are familiar with the intellectual history of the contemporary Church, which I outlined in *Confronting the Pope of Suspicion*, it's easy to understand how the Church came to this tragic place. For decades now, the Church of the Apostolic Creed has been undermined and, ultimately, usurped by a false and illegitimate church of "science" (*pseudoscience* really). In short, what we have is a mass apostasy in the hierarchy of the Church. And it is being led by the current occupant of the Chair of Peter.

Whom to turn to for leadership? That is the essential question. For the American Church, let me offer a partial answer in the negative. It most certainly is not Bishop Robert Barron of Los Angeles.

Confronting Robert Barron—Bishop of Suspicion

Barron was a keynote speaker at the 2018 World Meeting of Families in Dublin, a Vatican sponsored *Amoris Laetitia* conference. Despite Barron's constant evasions, his presentation at the conference hit every major talking point of the sexual liberation heresy. At midway through his talk, he repeated the German heresy found in chapter seven of *Amoris Laetitia* that sexual morality needs to be informed by science.[118] Nowhere in Barron's talk did he defend the *actual* teaching of the Church that our sexual morality comes, not from "science," but from the Bible. Like the heretics, Barron described the Bible's sexual morality as an "ideal" that not everyone can be expected to live up to.[119] This is a direct contradiction of the teaching of Church and Scripture which asserts that sexual morality is not a high ideal but, rather, a minimum standard for salvation, for a state of grace, and for access to the sacrament of Holy Communion.[120]

Gay Inclusion Based on Mercy? Or Equality?

Confronting the Pope of Suspicion

The centerpiece of sexual liberation theology, however, was *inclusion*, and Bishop Barron defended this in his talk as well. It is a heresy that rejects the Bible's minimum standards for a state of grace and access to Holy Communion. Because science supposedly demonstrated homosexuality to be normal, and the sexual prohibitions in the Bible invalid, there was no good reason to exclude persons who did not conform to Biblical sexual norms. If homosexuality is just as natural and healthy as heterosexuality, then, on what basis could one justify excluding gays from Holy Communion? As I described in CPS, a principal goal of the sexual liberationist was to bring gays into full communion and participation in the Church. And that full communion included reception of the Eucharist.[121] According to seventies radicals, gay inclusion was the logical consequence of gay equality which science was credited with establishing. As radical as that conclusion may seem, really it was the only reasonable conclusion to draw once one accepted the erroneous premise that science made gay okay.[122]

In his defense of inclusion, Barron was following paragraph 305 of *Amoris Laetitia*. It was there that Pope Francis recommended inclusion for persons who do not conform to the Church's sexual teachings. In a now notorious footnote, number 351, Pope Francis suggested that those living in irregular sexual situations should be allowed to receive Holy Communion. Somehow, this note was translated narrowly to mean that he was permitting the sacraments to couples living in adulterous relationships. Indeed he was. But he was doing so much more than that. He was also opening the sacraments to unrepentant homosexuals.[123] Anyone familiar with the sexual liberation heresy should have recognized it immediately in the pages of *Amoris Laetitia*. And in that context, note 351 was not shocking at all. It was inevitable.

The trick of course was in trying to sell this heresy to a laity that was too smart and too well schooled in the faith, much of the credit for that belonging to the heroic evangelization efforts of Mother Angelica and EWTN. This was Barron's assignment—to sell these heresies to the orthodox and faithful Mother Angelica crowd. And a Herculean task it was. The key to success would be in presenting a diluted version of gay inclusion. *Amoris Laetitia* was helpful in this regard. For it offered, not one, but two distinct arguments for gay inclusion: the real argument, which I just described, which asserts gay equality based on "science;" and a fake, watered-down version that was to be used for public relations purposes.

Both Francis and Barron prefer to emphasize the fake version. This version of gay inclusion treads lightly on the subject of full participation in the sacraments; hence the relegation of the suggestion to a footnote (351) in *Amoris Laetitia*. But it avoids altogether the incendiary assertions concerning science and gay equality which amount to full blown doctrinal heresy. Instead it emphasizes mercy and compassion: We ought to support gay inclusion at our parishes because it's the *nice* thing to do—*kinder, and more compassionate. It's what Jesus would do.* Then we are assured *falsely* that none of this amounts to any change in *doctrine*, but is only a *pastoral* shift toward a more compassionate and *Christian* inclusiveness.[124] The problem with this narrative is that it's a big lie. And Mundelein Seminary exposes that lie.

Gay Equality at Mundelein Seminary

As I pointed out in my book, there were no original ideas in *Amoris Laetitia*; thus gay inclusion too was an old idea. When Barron came to the topic of inclusion in his presentation, he raised the subject of Mundelein Seminary.[125] This was providential. For Mundelein was an early laboratory for gay inclusion. Barron had a long association with the seminary, first as a student, later as a professor, and ultimately as rector of the seminary.[126] What Mundelein demonstrates is that gay inclusion means gay equality—equal participation, equal access to the sacraments. It was one of Mundelein's trailblazing professors who co-authored the bible for sexual liberation theology. Her name was Sr. Agnes Cunningham, and the book was *Human Sexuality*, a book that enjoys the dubious distinction of having been condemned, not once, but twice, by two different popes.[127] She taught at Mundelein for twenty-four years, including the time that Barron spent there as a student.[128] Here is what the she wrote about Holy Communion for homosexuals:

> Christian homosexuals have the same needs and rights to the sacraments as heterosexuals....
> In the light of all these considerations, solidly probable opinion can be invoked in favor of permitting a homosexual ... free access to the sacraments of reconciliation and the Eucharist.[129]

Mundelein became a laboratory for all of the wild ideas in Cunningham's book, gay inclusion chief among them. It was an inclusion based, not on mercy for sinners, but on an equality that had been established by the sciences according to Cunningham's heretical book. Bishop Barron knew from his own experience that it wasn't out of "mercy and compassion" that gays were full participants at Mundelein. That would be to receive gays as you would receive a drug addict or wife-beater—as a sinner. No, gays were not second-class citizens in any respect. According to the excellent Michael Rose book *Goodbye, Good Men*, the gays ran the place at Mundelein. They were "out, proud, and open."[130]

The Barron and Francis propaganda that gay inclusion is based on compassion for sinners carries

Confronting the Pope of Suspicion

with it the implication that the sin of homosexuality is still recognized and that efforts should be made to repent or reform. But there was no repentance or reform at Mundelein because no one saw a need for it since *"science showed that homosexuality was normal and healthy."* And the same goes for all the seminaries around the world that practiced gay inclusion. If gay inclusion really was a pastoral policy to help gays overcome their sins and better conform themselves to the *"ideal of the Gospel,"* then where are all the books documenting the successes of these seminaries in converting their gay seminarians? You won't find any because they don't exist—because it never happened.

Just the opposite happened, in fact, as Michael Rose documents in his book. Seminarians at Mundelein weren't conforming to the Gospel; they were queering to their own disordered natures:

> "[T]here were madams, pimps, and prostitutes all in a major seminary system that, from the outside, if you were to walk through, would look very holy." Wurst added that "a large number of students had been convinced by some liberal teachers that sexual promiscuity with the same sex was not a violation of celibacy," an outrageous distortion of Catholic teaching. Those who would hope that things may have turned around at Mundelein since

> Wurst's days will be disappointed. Joseph Kellenyi, a seminarian at the Chicago-area seminary during the 1998–99 school year, confirmed that Wurst's portrait of the sexual immorality and shenanigans remains unchanged at the dawn of the twenty-first century. "I won't go so far as to say that some of the members of the formation team at Mundelein were literally 'pimps,' but one or two in particular certainly facilitated Chicago priests meeting the 'cute' seminarians." Kellenyi wondered why these priests would be interested in being introduced to certain seminarians who were favorites—and therefore "recommended" by openly gay faculty members. "One hall in the seminary dorm," related Kellenyi, "is nicknamed the 'Catwalk,' known as the residence of the more fashionable gays. . . . Oddly enough, attested Kellenyi, once a seminarian "came out," he would be wined and dined—literally—by certain faculty priests. . . . [T]he special status given to openly gay seminarians, he said, is beyond the pale.[131]

Let's not overlook the important lesson to be learned from Mundelein, which is this: The history of gay inclusion as it was taught and practiced by priests and seminarians over the past fifty years reveals that the point of gay inclusion was *never* to

Confronting the Pope of Suspicion

facilitate gay conversions. It was just the opposite—to assert gay *equality*—an equality that doesn't seek conversion at all because it doesn't recognize any need for conversion or repentance. On the contrary, it asserts gay equality on the grounds that science discovered homosexuality to be perfectly healthy, natural, and thus, not sinful or disordered in any way. To quote a popular James Martin refrain, "God made you the way you are; and you are beautifully and wonderfully made."

Church developments since the publication of *Amoris Laetitia* strongly suggest that the papal document is being read by the clergy as a green light for gay equality. That's what James Martin preaches, and he enjoys the support of many bishops.[132] The statements coming from the German Synod and the other events of the "December Massacre"—from the Vatican and the pope himself—all suggest that gay inclusion today is exactly what it was in progressive seminaries fifty years ago: Gay inclusion was never about facilitating gay conversions. It has always been about asserting gay equality.[133]

Thus, Barron's presentation on inclusion was a deception. True, it was a faithful presentation of paragraph 305 of Amoris, but that paragraph is, itself, a Trojan horse whose sole purpose is to deceive the faithful about the true nature of gay inclusion. The purpose of the deception? To spread gay inclusion and impose gay equality throughout the

Church with as little resistance as possible. More on that in a moment.

※ ※ ※

Fr. Richard John Neuhaus and *Human Sexuality*

As I explained in *Confronting the Pope of Suspicion*, there is yet an even darker lesson to be learned from the progressive culture at Mundelein. The heretical teaching that sexual morality should come from science rather than the Bible, and which Barron defended, albeit in a diluted form, was the chief cause of the sexual abuse crisis. As I showed in my book, it wasn't just homosexuality that was normalized. Some textbooks even defended pedophilia. These theology books cited "scientific" research that purported to demonstrate that pedophilia was not harmful to children.[134]

Although you won't hear it from Bishop Barron or Pope Francis or James Martin, you will hear it from Fr. Richard John Neuhaus that the sexual liberationist ideas of the seventies were directly responsible for the epidemic of clergy sexual abuse. In this 2002 excerpt from *First Things*, published in the midst of the exploding sex abuse scandal, Neuhaus specifically blames the Mundelein professor's textbook:

In 1972, the Catholic Theological Society

of America (CTSA) established a commission whose findings were published in a 1979 book from Doubleday, *Human Sexuality*. The seeds of everything that has come to light in recent months are to be found there....

The book is thoroughly revisionist from A to Z, flying in the face of the Church's teaching on contraception, celibacy, chastity, homosexuality, and even "albeit more delicately"on bestiality.... But the book has been widely used in seminaries. Seminarians and priests of the time who had a woman or a male lover on the side could, and did, cite *Human Sexuality* to reasonably claim that a very large part, if not the majority, of the academic theological establishment countenanced their behavior....

Thus did academic and theological dissent promiscuously issue permission slips for an era of wink-wink, nudge-nudge, the consequences of which are now on scandalous public display.[135]

Lessons From Bishop Barron

I made Bishop Barron the focus of this essay because, despite his many evasions and misrepresentations—and *because* of them—his defense of *Amoris Laetitia* was quite instructive. In his presentation Barron identified *and defended* the major ideas (and heresies) of *Amoris Laetitia*:[136]

- The heresy that science, and not the Bible, is the basis for understanding sexual morality; (This leads to the justification of homosexuality and other perversions like pedophilia. As I showed in *Confronting the Pope of Suspicion*, the science heresy was directly responsible for the clergy sexual abuse scandal.)
- The heresy that Biblical sexual morality is an ideal to strive for (or not) rather than a minimum standard for a state of grace and admission to Holy Communion;[137]
- The heresy, per note 351 of Amoris, recommending admission to Holy Communion for those who *"fall short of the Gospel ideal on sexuality,"* which violates the teaching on mortal sin. (This is the "gay inclusion" heresy.)

Barron's defense of *Amoris Laetitia* could have just as easily been a defense of the condemned Mundelein textbook *Human Sexuality*. They contain all the same heresies. As I explained in *Confronting the Pope of Suspicion*, all the ideas of *Amoris Laetitia* originated in the sexual liberation heresies of the seventies. Which explains why Barron thought to mention Mundelein in his commentary on gay inclusion. The connection that Barron makes between the teaching and practice of Mundelein and *Amoris Laetitia* proves that the clergy view Amoris in precisely this way: as a papal endorsement of these sexual liberation heresies. That's how Fr. James Martin reads *Amoris Laetitia*. And that's how the German bishops read it too. Which is how the dubia Cardinals also read the document and why they implicitly condemned it as contrary to Scripture and Tradition. And it goes without saying that, if Francis has *dubia* (questions) to answer for *Amoris Laetitia*, so do Bishop Barron and all the others who have promoted its heresies. The biggest dubium of all being the one coming from Fr. Richard John Neuhaus: how can a pope and so many bishops be promoting the very same ideas that were responsible for clergy sexual abuse?[138]

The Final Lesson of Mundelein: Gay Inclusion Became Gay Fascism.

On December 27, 2020, Francis declared 2021 to be a year of reflection on *Amoris Laetitia*. As I pointed out at the beginning of this essay, it will be a year of promotion and implementation. Thus, it will be a year of promotion and implementation of gay inclusion at dioceses all around the world. If you have read my book and this concluding postscript, it should not be a mystery to you what an era of gay inclusion will look like. It will look like Mundelein Seminary and all the other seminaries that have been practicing gay inclusion for decades. And that's a very bad thing. For the gay activists in seminaries did not practice the "mercy and compassion" that they preach. Instead, they tolerated no dissent against their policies of gay inclusion and equality. They denied to orthodox, faithful Catholics the right to freedom of conscience that they demand for themselves and for their allies. Anyone who dared to oppose the wicked heresy of gay equality was black-balled or thrown out of seminary, as Michael Rose described in his excellent book:

> Too often men who support the teachings of the Church, especially the teachings on sexual morality, are dismissed for being "rigid and uncharitable homophobes," while those seminarians who reject the Church's teaching or "come out" as gays to their superiors are given preferential treatment and then ordained to the Catholic priesthood.
>
> . . . .
>
> In short, many have hijacked the priesthood in order to change the Catholic Church from within. . . . The fact is that many qualified candidates for the priesthood have been turned away for political reasons over the past three decades. Systematic, ideological discrimination has been practiced against seminarians who uphold Catholic teaching on sexuality and other issues; dissenters from Catholic teaching—including teaching on homosexuality—have been rewarded.[139]

In an era of cancel culture and liberal fascism, gay inclusion at your church will also include legions of gay lawyers and their gay media allies. Their gay congressional representatives. Their gay judges. If you so much as dare to whisper the Truth of the Gospel within the walls of your own Christian Church, you are about to meet an army of opposition. And they are legion.

"We Cannot Bless Sin"

On March 15, it was reported that Pope Francis had agreed with a Vatican ruling that the Church cannot bless same-sex weddings since God "cannot bless sin."[140] Try to imagine for a moment, in this era of liberal fascism, what would have happened if the pope ruled the other way. Lines would be around the block of gay activist fascists signing up for a gay marriage ceremony at the local Catholic Church. And you know who would be the best man and maid of honor? Their lawyers. Any pastor or bishop who dared to refuse would have been hit with a massive lawsuit. And not just one lawsuit. Hundreds. The media would descend like a pack of wolves. And the difficult question that any honest priest would be stuck answering is this: "What gives you the authority to defy the pope?" Make no mistake. We dodged a bullet this time. But this entire "Year of Reflection on *Amoris Laetitia*" will be like the Alamo, O.K. Corral, and St. Valentine's Day Massacre all rolled into one. This year of *implemen-*

tation of *Amoris Laetitia* threatens to become a year of extortion for our parishes: surrender to the gay fascists, or we'll turn your churches into Memories Pizza and Masterpiece Cakeshop.[141] We'll drag your leaders through the mud of our liberal media allies and get them fired from their jobs for the crime of being "homophobic bigots."

The Great Catholic Reset

As I stated at the beginning, this is not a year of *reflection*, but of promotion and *implementation*. And it has already begun. Dioceses around the world are making preparations. The Germans are calling for the Catechism to be changed on the subject of homosexuality.[142] In Brazil, the bishops included pro-LGBT themes and messages in their formal Lenten reflections for parishes.[143] Pope Francis and Cardinal Marx are calling for a new era to dawn.[144] It is an era of gay equality and liberation in the Church. Call it "The Great Gay Catholic Reset."

In my own diocese of Raleigh, and kept secret from the laity, a multi-parish, pro-LGBT Lenten Bible study is under way. It is being led by the St. Francis of Assisi parish in Raleigh—a parish with a long-standing LGBT ministry associated with the Raleigh Gay Pride Parade.[145] Participants include unsuspecting parishes that have never before supported any kind of pro-LGBT ministry. In fact, at one parish that I happen to know quite well, St.

Confronting the Pope of Suspicion

Andrew's, they actively resisted such efforts a few years ago and forced the removal of their heretical pastor.[146] But this year, in the year of implementation and extortion, gay liberation is being imposed on St. Andrew's without their knowledge and consent. I am informed by a reliable source that the plan is to use this initial Bible study to secretly impose permanent pro-LGBT ministries at St. Andrew's and other unsuspecting parishes in the diocese. My source tells me they are using this initial Bible study to identify leaders who can run these LGBT ministries. And while it is true that past efforts, like at St. Andrew's, have failed, this time is very different. This time they are organized and united.

Just like the gay liberation seminaries of the seventies, gay liberation and equality is being imposed on the orthodox faithful. In an uncanny reflection of societal trends in the West, leftist, gay totalitarianism in the Church is being exported from Catholic academia to the Catholic mainstream, to our local church communities. And just like the seminaries, there will be no freedom to opt out. Mark my words, the mercy and compassion that the LGBT community demands from us will not be reciprocated.[147]

Live Not By Lies

What is to be done then? This year of *Amoris Laetitia* has barely gotten off the ground, and that is a good thing for any resistance movement. Plans to implement LGBT ministries are only in their initial planning stages, and that is when a movement is at its weakest. So now is the best time to act, but what should our strategy be? Bishop Barron, again, is the key to our understanding. It is clear from his presentation that it was not his primary goal to instruct his audience. He stated that he was assigned to present on chapters seven through nine, but he tells the audience that he wants to just skip chapter eight, the most controversial.[148] Barron wasn't teaching *Amoris Laetitia*; he was selling it. And like a dishonest used car salesman, his plan was to hide the defects: *To tell lies.*

But it wasn't a car he was selling. It was a Trojan horse—stuffed with heretical German bishops and Jesuits. Pay close attention to Barron's presentation, and you will see that he praised and defended all the same things the German bishops praise, all the same heresies of the seventies that guided Mundelein Seminary. The connection is difficult to see clearly because Barron employs so many evasions and misrepresentations. *He tells lies.*

How do the fascists get you to conform, to get you to do their will rather than your own? One way they succeed is by telling lies—lies designed to make you believe that their will and your will are the same. And that takes some intellectual acrobatics, as the dystopian authors teach us:

- *War is peace.*
- *Freedom is slavery.*
- *Ignorance is strength.*
- *Science is infallible.*
- *Homosexuality is Christian.*
- *Jesus wants gays to take over your churches.*

Solzhenitsyn teaches us that the best way to fight totalitarianism is to *"live not by lies."*[149] I hope this little book can serve as a useful resource for doing just that.

✳ ✳ ✳

BIBLIOGRAPHY

American Association of University Professors. (1989, Sept–Oct). *Academic Freedom and Tenure: The Catholic University of America*. Retrieved May 12, 2019, from American Association of University Professors: **https://www.aaup.org/NR/rdonlyres/9CA4679F-7BC7-4AD7-BA37-0C1B00AEBAA1/0/CatholicUUSA.pdf**

Anonymous. (2018, May 14). *Priest Explains How Amoris Laetitia Was Really Written to 'Normalize' Homosexuality*. Retrieved April 30, 2019, from LifeSite News: https://www.lifesitenews.com/opinion/priest-explains-how-amoris-laetitia-was-really-written-to-normalize-homosex

Baklinski, P. (2016, November 24). *Francis Praises Major Humanae Vitae Dissenter in Rebuke of 'White or Black' Morality*. Retrieved April 30, 2019, from Life Site News: https://www.lifesitenews.com/news/francis-praises-prominent-humanae-vitae-dissenter-for-his-radical-new-moral

Becker, J. M. (1997). *The Re-Formed Jesuits, Volume II*

—*A History of Changes in Jesuit Formation During the Decade 1965–1975* (Vol. 2). San Francisco, CA, USA: Ignatius Press.

Becker, J. M. (1992). *The Re-Formed Jesuits, Volume I —A History of Changes in Jesuit Formation During the Decade 1965–1975* (Vol. 1). San Francisco, CA, USA: Ignatius Press.

Benedict XVI, P. E. (2019, April 10). *Full Text of Benedict XVI Essay: 'The Church and the Scandal of Sexual abuse'*. Retrieved May 7, 2019, from Catholic News Agency: https://www.catholicnewsagency.com/news/full-text-of-benedict-xvi-the-church-and-the-scandal-of-sexual-abuse-59639

Bernstein, C., & Politi, M. (1996). *His Holiness: John Paul II and the History of Our Time.* New York, NY, USA: Penguin Books.

Catholic Resource Network—Trinity Communications. (1994). *"We Overcame Their Traditions, We Overcame Their Faith"*. Retrieved from EWTN: https://www.ewtn.com/library/PRIESTS/COULSON.TXT

Chretien, C. (2017, April 12). *Vatican Names Pro-Gay Fr. James Martin as Communications Consultant* . Retrieved May 21, 2019, from Life Site News: https://www.lifesitenews.com/news/pope-francis-picks-pro-gay-jesuit-as-consultant-for-vatican-communications

CNA Staff. (2016, April 8). *No Doctrine Change*

From Pope Francis – but a Call for Better Pastoral Care. Retrieved May 14, 2019, from Catholic News Agency: https://www.catholicnewsagency.com/news/no-doctrine-change-from-pope-francis-but-a-call-for-better-pastoral-care-85474

Coulson, W. (1994). Full Hearts and Empty Heads: The Price of Certain Recent Programs in Humanistic Psychology. *The Nature and Tasks of a Personalistic Psychology.* Steubenville: Franciscan University of Steubenville: http://www.ewtn.com/library/academic/fullhear.htm

Cozzens, D. B. (2000). *The Changing Face of the Priesthood—A Reflection on the Priest's Crisis of Soul.* Collegeville, MN, USA: Liturgical Press.

CultureShockTV. (2011, May 21). *Psychologist William R. Coulson: The Goal Was to Replace Religion With Psychology*. Retrieved April 27, 2019, from YouTube: https://www.youtube.com/watch?v=90ZfGBHkA_0

Curran, C. (1998, July 17). *Bernard Häring: A Moral Theologian Whose Soul Matched His Scholarship*. Retrieved May 3, 2019, from National Catholic Reporter: http://natcath.org/NCR_Online/archives2/1998c/071798/071898h.htm

Emerson, R. W. (1949). Self-Reliance. In R. W. Emerson, *Selected Essays* (pp. 29–59). Chicago, IL, USA: The Fountain Press.

Foy, V. (2014, January 8). *Tragedy at Winnipeg: The*

Canadian Catholic Bishops' Statement on Humanae Vitae". Retrieved April 30, 2019, from MsgrFoy.Com: https://msgrfoy.com/2014/01/08/tragedy-at-winnipeg-the-canadian-catholic-bishops-statement-on-humanae-vitae-by-monsignor-vincent-foy/

Francis, P. (2015). *The Joy of Love—Amoris Laetitia.* Boston, MA, USA: Beacon Publishing.

Freud, S. (1961). *Civilization and Its Discontents.* (J. Strachey, Trans.) New York, NY, USA: W.W. Norton & Company.

Gramick, J., & DeBernardo, F. (2012, February 14). A Catholic Case for Same-Sex Marriage. *Washington Post*.

Gravino, J. (2018, September 12). *How Neuroscience Explains Sex Abuse and Vindicates ... Prayer and Fasting.* Retrieved May 15, 2019, from The Stream: https://stream.org/how-neuroscience-explains-sex-abuse-and-vindicates-prayer-and-fasting/

Gravino, J. (2018, March 14). *The Cause of Declining Violence—Enlightenment? Or Incarceration?* Retrieved May 15, 2019, from New Walden: https://newwalden.org/2018/03/14/the-cause-of-declining-violence-enlightenment-or-incarceration/

Gravino, J. (2015). *The Immoral Landscape of the New Atheism.* Apex, NC, USA: Amazon.

Guindon, A. (1976). *The Sexual Language—An Essay in Moral Theology.* Ottawa, Ontario, Canada: The University of Ottawa Press.

Harlan, C., & Pitrelli, S. (2019, April 11). Ex-Pope Benedict Contradicts Pope Francis in Unusual Intervention on Sexual Abuse. *Washington Post*.

Hickson, M. (2019, March 29). *Evidence Pope Follows Blueprint to Change Church by Dissident Cardinal Who Led St. Gallen 'Mafia'*. Retrieved May 14, 2019, from Life Site News: https://www.lifesitenews.com/blogs/evidence-pope-follows-blueprint-to-change-church-by-dissident-cardinal-who-led-st.-gallen-mafia

John Paul II, P. (1997). *Man and Woman He Created Them—A Theology of the Body.* Boston, MA, USA: Pauline Books & Media.

John Paul II, P. (1993). *The Splendor of Truth: Veritatis Splendor.* Boston, MA, USA: St. Paul Books & Media.

Jones, E. M. (1999, October). *Carl Rogers and the IHM Nuns: Sensitivity Training, Psychological Warfare and the "Catholic Problem"*. Retrieved May 9, 2019, from Culture Wars: http://www.culturewars.com/CultureWars/1999/rogers.html

Jung, C. (1933). *Modern Man in Search of a Soul.* (W. Dell, & C. F. Baynes, Trans.) New York, NY, USA: Harcourt Brace Jovanovich.

Kosnick, A., Carroll, W., Cunningham, A., Modras, R., & Schulte, J. (1977). *Human Sexuality: New Directions in American Catholic Thought.* New York, NY, USA: Paulist Press.

Lobdell, W. (2004, January 10). Celibacy Requirement Doesn't Work, Ex-Monk Says. *Los Angeles Times*.

Martin, J. (2017). *Building a Bridge—How the Catholic Church and the LGBT Community Can Enter into a Relationship of Respect, Compassion, and Sensitivity.* New York, NY, USA: HarperCollins.

Nietzsche, F. (1956). *The Genealogy of Morals.* (F. Golffing, Trans.) Garden City, NY, USA: Doubleday & Company, Inc.

Pakaluk, M. (2017, January 15). *Ethicist Says Ghostwriter's Role in 'Amoris' Is Troubling.* Retrieved April 30, 2019, from Crux: https://cruxnow.com/commentary/2017/01/15/ethicist-says-ghostwriters-role-amoris-troubling/

Paul VI, P. (1968). *Humanae Vitae: A Challenge to Love.* New Hope, Kentucky, USA: New Hope Publications.

Pentin, E. (2016, November 14). *Full Text and Explanatory Notes of Cardinals' Questions on 'Amoris Laetitia'.* Retrieved April 30, 2019, from National Catholic Register: http://www.ncregister.com/blog/edward-pentin/full-text-and-explanatory-notes-of-cardinals-questions-on-amoris-laetitia

Pentin, E. (2015). *The Rigging of a Vatican Synod?* San Francisco, CA, USA: Ignatius Press.

Podles, L. J. (2008). *Sacrilege: Sexual Abuse in the Catholic Church.* Baltimore, MD, USA: Crossland Press.

Rose, M. S. (2002). *Goodbye, Good Men—How Liberals Brought Corruption Into the Catholic Church.* Washington, DC, USA: Regnery Publishing.

Schneiders, S. (1978). Vow (Practice And Theology). *New Catholic Encyclopedia—Supplement: Change in the Church*, xvii, 696–699.

Sciambra, J. (2017, September 16). *"Why Not?"—James Martin Thinks Gay Men Should Be Able to Kiss in Church.* Retrieved April 29, 2019, from YouTube: https://www.youtube.com/watch?time_continue=2&v=xa2DXkw7Xuc

Sciambra, J. (2017, June 9). *James Martin: Jesus Says Nothing About Homosexuality.* Retrieved May 13, 2019, from YouTube: https://www.youtube.com/watch?time_continue=1&v=cXAXlxAdbGQ

Skojec, S. (2017, October 18). *Program for 2018 World Meeting of Families Features Homosexual Imagery and Themes.* Retrieved April 30, 2019, from One Peter Five: https://onepeterfive.com/program-2018-world-meeting-families-features-homosexual-imagery-themes/

Soane, B. (1977). The Literature of Medical Ethics: Bernard Haring. *Journal of Medical Ethics*, 3, 85–92.

Sullins, D. P. (2018). *Report: Clergy Sex Abuse.* Retrieved April 27, 2019, from Ruth Institute: http://www.ruthinstitute.org/clergy-sex-abuse-statistical-analysis

Tanner, H. (1979, December 9). Vatican Condemns Book by U.S. Priests; Denounces Liberal Sexual Attitude Contained in 2-Year-Old Work. *New York Times*.

Terry, K. S. (2011). *The Causes and Context of Sexual Abuse of Minors by Catholic Priests in the United States, 1950–2010.* John Jay College Research Team. Washington, D.C.: United States Conference of Catholic Bishops.

Thevathasan, P. (2017, March). *Bernard Häring and his Medical Ethics.* (Christendom Awake) Retrieved May 13, 2019, from Catholic Culture: https://www.catholicculture.org/culture/library/view.cfm?recnum=11510

Varacalli, J. A. (n.d.). *Obstructing Ex Corde Ecclesiae.* Retrieved May 21, 2019, from Catholic Culture: https://www.catholicculture.org/culture/library/view.cfm?recnum=2703

Vatican. (2014, October 15). *Relatio Post Disceptationem for 2014 Synod of Bishops on the Family.* Retrieved April 30, 2019, from National Catholic Reporter: https://www.ncronline.org/news/vatican/relatio-post-disceptationem-2014-synod-bishops-family

Weigel, G. (1999). *Witness to Hope: The Biography of Pope John Paul II.* New York, New York, USA: HarperCollins.

✻ ✻ ✻

NOTES

[1] http://www.ncregister.com/blog/edward-pentin/full-text-and-explanatory-notes-of-cardinals-questions-on-amoris-laetitia

[2] https://stream.org/the-vaticans-alliance-with-china-more-evil-than-we-thought/

[3] (Benedict XVI, 2019) See online: https://www.catholicnewsagency.com/news/full-text-of-benedict-xvi-the-church-and-the-scandal-of-sexual-abuse-59639

[4] (Harlan & Pitrelli, 2019) See online: https://www.washingtonpost.com/world/speaking-out-at-this-difficult-hour-a-once-quiet-ex-pope-pens-a-lengthy-letter-on-sexual-abuse/2019/04/11/0ffa162e-5c1a-11e9-a00e-050dc7b82693_story.html?utm_term=.dc1981dbba78

[5] (Sullins, 2018, pp. 10–21) Sullins gives the question about the prevalence of current clergy sexual abuse an extensive treatment in his report. He correctly points out that current abuse is difficult to

track because often, and especially in the case of child victims, sexual abuse is not reported until years, or even decades, after the offense took place. Nevertheless, some data suggests that numbers are going up. Note, especially, figure 7 on page 20.

[6] This is not ultimately about celibacy or homosexuality, the two favorite theories of the pundit class depending on one's political leanings. Ending clerical celibacy and purging the priesthood of homosexuals will not end the crisis of sexual abuse. And the simplest proof of this is to be found in the Baptist church. In a church comprised almost entirely of married, heterosexual ministers, they are reeling from a sexual abuse crisis of their own. Hence, the idea that a married heterosexual priesthood is going to solve anything is preposterous. What is needed is a better theory. For that we need to do a little research.

[7] (John Paul II, Man and Woman He Created Them—A Theology of the Body, 1997, pp. 309–314)

[8] (Emerson, 1949, p. 34–35)

[9] (John Paul II, Man and Woman He Created Them—A Theology of the Body, 1997, p. 281)

[10] The masters' critique was not new. In fact, it was almost as old as the Church itself, well known to the Church as the heresy of Pelagianism, a natural enough objection that has taken different forms

over the centuries (http://www.newadvent.org/cathen/11604a.htm).

[11] (Nietzsche, 1956, pp. 280–281)

[12] (Freud, 1961, p. 109)

[13] (Freud, 1961, pp. 60–61)

[14] (Jung, 1933, p. 230)

[15] (Becker, The Re-Formed Jesuits, Volume II—A History of Changes in Jesuit Formation During the Decade 1965–1975, 1997, pp. 127–128)

[16] (Schneiders, 1978, p. 697, col.1)

[17] (Schneiders, 1978, p. 697, col. 1)

[18] (Schneiders, 1978, p. 697, col. 1)

[19] (Becker, The Re-Formed Jesuits, Volume I—A History of Changes in Jesuit Formation During the Decade 1965–1975, 1992, pp. 173–175)

[20] (Schneiders, 1978, p. 698, col. 1)

[21] (Schneiders, 1978, p. 698, col. 1)

[22] (Schneiders, 1978, p. 697, col. 2) "There is increasing discussion of the possibility that not every religious profession need be perpetual."

[23] (Lobdell, 2004) This is a book review of *Celibacy in Crisis: A Secret World Revisited* by Richard Sipe. The article quotes from Sipe's book:

> "The church 'is using Scripture as a basis for explaining the science of human sexuality,' Sipe writes in *Celibacy in Crisis*.... 'That is no more valid than using the Bible to explain cosmology.'"

[24] (Becker, The Re-Formed Jesuits, Volume I—A History of Changes in Jesuit Formation During the Decade 1965–1975, 1992, p. 171)

[25] (Becker, The Re-Formed Jesuits, Volume I—A History of Changes in Jesuit Formation During the Decade 1965–1975, 1992, p. 248)

[26] (Becker, The Re-Formed Jesuits, Volume I—A History of Changes in Jesuit Formation During the Decade 1965–1975, 1992, p. 248)

[27] (Becker, The Re-Formed Jesuits, Volume I—A History of Changes in Jesuit Formation During the Decade 1965–1975, 1992, p. 249)

[28] (Becker, The Re-Formed Jesuits, Volume I—A History of Changes in Jesuit Formation During the Decade 1965–1975, 1992, pp. 249–252)

[29] (Catholic Resource Network—Trinity Communications, 1994) online: https://www.ewtn.com/library/PRIESTS/COULSON.TXT

[30] (Catholic Resource Network—Trinity Communications, 1994) online: https://www.ewtn.com/library/PRIESTS/COULSON.TXT

[31] (Catholic Resource Network—Trinity Communications, 1994) online: https://www.ewtn.com/library/PRIESTS/COULSON.TXT

[32] (Jones, 1999) See online: http://www.culturewars.com/CultureWars/1999/rogers.html This is an excerpt from Jones's book, Libido Dominandi: Sexual Liberation and Political Control

[33] (Catholic Resource Network—Trinity Communications, 1994) online: https://www.ewtn.com/library/PRIESTS/COULSON.TXT

[34] (Catholic Resource Network—Trinity Communications, 1994) online: https://www.ewtn.com/library/PRIESTS/COULSON.TXT

[35] (Catholic Resource Network—Trinity Communications, 1994) online: https://www.ewtn.com/library/PRIESTS/COULSON.TXT

[36] (Catholic Resource Network—Trinity Communications, 1994) online: https://www.ewtn.com/library/PRIESTS/COULSON.TXT

[37] (Catholic Resource Network—Trinity Communications, 1994) online: https://www.ewtn.com/library/PRIESTS/COULSON.TXT

[38] (Podles, 2008; See online excerpt: http://www.renewamerica.com/columns/abbott/100124); Podles's account is corroborated by Coulson himself in an address at Franciscan University: (Coulson, 1994; See online: http://www.ewtn.com/library/academic/fullhear.htm)

[39] (CultureShockTV, 2011) See online: https://www.youtube.com/watch?v=90ZfGBHkA_0

[40] Two excellent books that document the disappearance of celibacy in seminary life: (Rose, 2002) (Podles, 2008)

[41] (Schneiders, 1978)

[42] (Sullins, 2018, pp. 25–31) See online: https://spark.adobe.com/page/xIVdVcuq9whJL/

[43] (Terry, 2011, p. 62) See online: http://www.usccb.org/issues-and-action/child-and-youth-protection/upload/the-causes-and-context-of-sexual-abuse-of-minors-by-catholic-priests-in-the-united-states-1950-2010.pdf

[44] (Kosnick, Carroll, Cunningham, Modras, & Schulte, 1977, pp. 96–98) On page 97, we are told that specific laws against "masturbation, sterilization, contraception, [and] premarital sex ... cannot be regarded as universal and absolute moral norms." They are just "guidelines."

[45] (Kosnick, Carroll, Cunningham, Modras, &

Schulte, 1977, p. 56–57)

[46] (Kosnick, Carroll, Cunningham, Modras, & Schulte, 1977) on bestiality: p. 61; on incest: p. 60

[47] (Kosnick, Carroll, Cunningham, Modras, & Schulte, 1977, p. 56)

[48] A universal feature of the dissenting theologies is their *faux* enthusiasm for Vatican II. *Human Sexuality* is no exception. Like the other progressive works, HS takes great pains to link its errors to Vatican II. On page 96, for example, HS claims that its first universal principle of moral reasoning comes from *Gaudium et Spes 51.* GS 51 essentially asserts a natural law formulation of morality, namely, that the moral law is derived from human nature. *Human Sexuality* agrees with this much. However, GS 51 also declares that this human nature of man necessarily includes a supernatural dimension that we learn about from divine revelation. It includes the belief that man possesses an immortal soul with an eternal destiny. But HS, true to its master-of-suspicion-form, rejects a theologically informed concept of human nature as naïve, (p. 54), and it attempts to derive an understanding of human nature exclusively from the sciences. For if it had included an understanding of the soul and man's eternal destiny, it would have understood that incest and bestiality, along with homosexuality, adultery, etc. are inimical to man's final end. The point, here, is that HS does not really follow

Vatican II. It simply uses Vatican II as an orthodox camouflage to conceal its heresies. HS claims to be following GS 51, but in reality it rejects it. This is a consistent pattern with progressives: they embrace the "spirit" of Vatican II, whatever that means, but reject its letter. Some conservatives unfortunately fall for this hustle and are thus led into thinking *erroneously* that Vatican II is the source of progressive heterodoxy. It isn't. The true source of practically all progressive error is a social-science-inspired modernism.

[49] (Tanner, 1979) See online: https://www.nytimes.com/1979/12/09/archives/vatican-condemns-book-by-us-priests-denounces-liberal-sexual.html

[50] (Bernstein & Politi, 1996, pp. 416–422) Although sympathetic to the dissenters, nevertheless, Bernstein's account provides important details of the controversies. See also (Weigel, 1999, pp. 523–525). See also (Catholic Resource Network—Trinity Communications, 1994), online: https://www.ewtn.com/library/PRIESTS/COULSON.TXT. The story of the Jesuits in this interview is appalling. William Coulson describes the Jesuit "Third Way." According to Coulson, the "Third Way" amounted to a justification of fornication for priests. In their gratitude to Rogers for liberating their sexuality, the Jesuits, says Coulson, awarded Rogers two honorary doctorates.

[51] (Varacalli) See online: https://www.catholicculture.org/culture/library/view.cfm?recnum=2703

[52] (Sciambra, 2017) See online: https://www.youtube.com/watch?time_continue=2&v=xa2DXkw7Xuc

[53] (Martin, 2017) See, for example, the epigraph, which quotes psalm 139: 13–14.

[54] (Martin, 2017, p. 52)

[55] (Martin, 2017, pp. 46–47)

[56] (Chretien, 2017) See online: https://www.lifesitenews.com/news/pope-francis-picks-pro-gay-jesuit-as-consultant-for-vatican-communications

[57] (Skojec, 2017) See online: https://onepeterfive.com/program-2018-world-meeting-families-features-homosexual-imagery-themes/

[58] (Anonymous, 2018) See online: https://www.lifesitenews.com/opinion/priest-explains-how-amoris-laetitia-was-really-written-to-normalize-homosex

[59] (Vatican, 2014) See online: https://www.ncronline.org/news/vatican/relatio-post-disceptationem-2014-synod-bishops-family

[60] (Pentin, 2015) See chapter 1 and the conclusion.

[61] (Pentin, Full Text and Explanatory Notes of Cardinals' Questions on 'Amoris Laetitia', 2016) See online: http://www.ncregister.com/blog/edward-pentin/full-text-and-explanatory-notes-of-cardinals-questions-on-amoris-laetitia

[62] Paragraph 304 of AL also denies the concept of an absolute moral norm that could be applied to irregular sexual situations.

[63] In a papal document that recommends situational ethics for irregular sexual relationships, what an egregious omission to fail to clearly define the boundaries and limitations of such a theory, namely, that Church teaching regarding absolute moral norms must always be respected. In fact, *Amoris Laetitia* does the opposite. The concept of absolute moral norms is consistently *criticized* in multiple places all throughout the document. But not in a single place can one find a word of criticism for situational ethics. In reading AL and comparing it to the dissenting theologies of the twentieth century, one struggles to find any difference.

[64] This is not the first accusation of plagiarism against *Amoris Laetitia.* See here for another: (Pakaluk, 2017). Pakaluk's accusation concerns different passages from AL, however.

[65] (Kosnick, Carroll, Cunningham, Modras, & Schulte, 1977, p. 98)

[66] (Tanner, 1979) See online: http://www.vatican.va/roman_curia/congregations/cfaith/documents/rc_con_cfaith_doc_19790713_mons-quinn_en.html

[67] These guidelines are found in the Canadian Bishops' notorious "Winnipeg Statement."

[68] (Foy, 2014) See online: https://msgrfoy.com/2014/01/08/tragedy-at-winnipeg-the-canadian-catholic-bishops-statement-on-humanae-vitae-by-monsignor-vincent-foy/

[69] (American Association of University Professors, 1989) See online: https://www.aaup.org/NR/rdonlyres/9CA4679F-7BC7-4AD7-BA37-0C1B00AEBAA1/0/CatholicUUSA.pdf

[70] (Baklinski, 2016) See online: https://www.lifesitenews.com/news/francis-praises-prominent-humanae-vitae-dissenter-for-his-radical-new-moral

[71] (Francis, 2015) The word "discernment" shows up 32 times in *Amoris Laetitia*. Paragraph 37 is typical of the way the word is used throughout the document: Discernment of complex situations is the work that individual consciences are expected to carry out. This discernment is contrasted with a "doctrinal, bioethical" approach at the beginning of par. 37. But it is in chapter eight, which begins at paragraph 291 and deals with "irregular situations,"

where Francis' discernment is indistinguishable from Häring's heretical sexual morality. In par. 293, "pastoral discernment of situations" is called for specifically in cases that deviate from the norms of Christian marriage.

Paragraph 296 introduces the section entitled "The Discernment of Irregular Situations." At par. 297, we are told that the goal of this discernment is to bring about universal inclusion and participation in the life of the Church. It emphasizes that this inclusion is not just for the divorced and remarried but for "everyone." Thus par. 297 is calling for a universal participation that includes *all irregular sexual situations*. Paragraph 299 continues the theme of inclusion. And then we come to the key paragraph—number 300. Paragraph 300 is the concluding paragraph of this section, and it is clear from its opening that it functions as a summary of this section:

"If we consider the immense variety of concrete situations <u>such as those I have mentioned</u>, it is understandable that neither the Synod nor this Exhortation could be expected to provide a new set of general rules, canonical in nature and applicable to all cases. What is possible is simply a renewed encouragement to undertake a responsible personal and pastoral discernment of particular cases ..."

So it is clear from the structure of AL that this conclusion is meant to apply to **all irregular sexual situations.** Thus the conclusion of paragraph 300 is

Confronting the Pope of Suspicion

heretical. As John Paul stated in *Veritatis Splendor*, par. 81, there are absolute moral norms governing sexuality, and this has always meant that some sexual acts are intrinsically evil. VS 81 clearly states that this is an apostolic teaching that the Church has always taught. Thus, the conclusion is heretical which states that there are no general rules that apply without exception in matters of sexual morality. This is **exactly** where exceptionless rules do apply according to the constant teaching of the Church.

Lumen Gentium, par. 25, makes it clear that the pope is obligated to conform to the teachings of revelation:

"Furthermore, when the Roman Pontiff, or the body of bishops together with him, define a doctrine, they make the definition in conformity with revelation itself, to which all are bound to adhere and to which they are obliged to submit.... The Roman Pontiff and the bishops, by reason of their office and the seriousness of the matter, apply themselves with zeal to the work of enquiring by every suitable means into this revelation and of giving apt expression to its contents; they do not, however, admit any new public revelation as pertaining to the divine deposit of faith."

Should it not be obvious to everyone that in fact there **are** general rules concerning irregular sexual situations that are in fact "applicable to all cases?" And should it not be equally obvious that these rules come from divine revelation and belong perpetually to the divine deposit of faith?

Thou shalt not commit adultery.

Should it not be obvious that no one—not even a pope—has the authority to set aside the Ten Commandments?

Thus, what paragraph 300 has accomplished is that it has established an heretical guideline for moral discernment and conscience formation which says that individual circumstances matter and rules don't because there are so many exceptions to the rules. (As is described below, *Amoris Laetitia* confirms this interpretation of par. 300 at par. 304. So, although there may be other readings of par. 300, they are not reasonable and not compatible with the AL text itself.)

The next section of chapter eight, beginning at paragraph 301, proceeds to the next logical step, which is to identify those situations and factors that can provide exceptions to the moral rules. It is fittingly titled, "Mitigating factors in Pastoral Discernment." What are some of the relevant factors?

Psychological factors are mentioned specifically. This is another troubling point of convergence with Häring, for Häring believed that psychological factors could overrule prohibitions against intrinsic evils. Do psychological factors play an identical role in *Amoris Laetitia*? Yes, they do. For it is precisely such factors as one's psychological constitution that make it impossible to formulate absolute moral norms that apply without exception (300 & 304). What exactly are these psychological factors? *Amoris Laetitia* doesn't say, but we have seen that other works that appear to have influenced AL offer more detail in this regard. Both the NCE and *Human Sexuality* cite psychological authorities to argue that homosexuality should be a morally accepted behavior—contrary to Scripture and Tradition. Such a position is transparently heretical, and it is a definite hazard to be avoided when theologians cast aside the Ten Commandments in favor of the latest pop-psychology fad. The psychological or scientific justification of homosexuality is promoted today by James Martin and his allies at New Ways Ministries who are campaigning to change the language of the Catechism (Martin, 2017, pp. 46–47) (Gramick & DeBernardo, 2012). *Amoris Laetitia* makes their heretical efforts much easier.

In the next and penultimate section of chapter eight, Francis provides clear confirmation of the above interpretation of *Amoris Laetitia* (and par.300). It is called "Rules and Discernment," and it begins at par. 304. At par. 304, he quotes Thomas Aquinas: "The principle will be found to fail, according as we descend into detail." From this, Francis draws the following heretical conclusion: "It is true that general rules set forth a good which can never be disregarded or neglected, *but in their formulation they cannot provide absolutely for all particular situations*." While this is certainly true of *some* rules, it is not true of *all* rules. Francis here has denied the possibility of absolute moral norms, which are exceptionless and which include the category of the intrinsic evils. It is a teaching of Sacred Scripture and Tradition that such absolute moral norms exist and that they govern sexual morality, as Pope St. John Paul the Great reminds us in *Veritatis Splendor* 81. Thus, in *Amoris Laetitia,* Francis has denied a most central teaching of Sacred Scripture and Tradition regarding sexual morality.

[72] (Baklinski, 2016) See online: https://www.lifesitenews.com/news/francis-praises-prominent-humanae-vitae-dissenter-for-his-radical-new-moral

[73] (Baklinski, 2016) See online: https://www.lifesitenews.com/news/francis-praises-prominent-humanae-vitae-dissenter-for-his-radical-new-moral

[74] A consistent theme in Francis' writings and statements is his criticism of rules. Nowhere can you find an explicit defense of absolute moral norms. Given that such norms belong to the deposit of revelation, as St. John Paul reminds us in *Veritatis Splendor,* this is a problem for the pope. He *appears* to be denying a teaching of divine revelation, and whether he is in fact doing this or not, even the ap-

pearance is unacceptable according to the teaching of *Lumen Gentium* 25. For LG 25 states that it is the pope's duty to give "apt expression" to revelation, which he has clearly failed to do if it appears to so many that he is in fact *denying* that revelation.

[75] (Baklinski, 2016) See online: https://www.lifesitenews.com/news/francis-praises-prominent-humanae-vitae-dissenter-for-his-radical-new-moral

[76] (Curran, 1998) See online: http://natcath.org/NCR_Online/archives2/1998c/071798/071898h.htm

[77] (Curran, 1998) See online: http://natcath.org/NCR_Online/archives2/1998c/071798/071898h.htm

[78] (Soane, 1977, p.87) See online: https://www.ncbi.nlm.nih.gov/pmc/articles/PMC1154560/pdf/jmedeth00171-0033.pdf

[79] Barbra Streisand recently spoke of the "sexual needs" of Michael Jackson to rationalize his alleged pedophilia. She was harshly criticized for her "humanistic" and very un-rigid approach to morality.

[80] (Thevathasan, 2017) See online: https://www.catholicculture.org/culture/library/view.cfm?recnum=11510

[81] (CultureShockTV, 2011) See online: https://

www.youtube.com/watch?time_continue=9&v=90ZfGBHkA_0

[82] (Gramick & DeBernardo, 2012) See online: https://www.washingtonpost.com/local/a-catholic-case-for-same-sex-marriage/2012/02/13/gIQAl4cwDR_story.html

[83] (Sciambra, James Martin: Jesus Says Nothing About Homosexuality, 2017) See online: https://www.youtube.com/watch?time_continue=1&v=cXAXlxAdbGQ

[84] (Podles, 2008) See online excerpt: http://www.renewamerica.com/columns/abbott/100124

[85] (Podles, 2008) See online: http://www.renewamerica.com/columns/abbott/100124

[86] (Podles, 2008) See online excerpt: http://www.renewamerica.com/columns/abbott/100124

[87] (Podles, 2008) See online excerpt: http://www.renewamerica.com/columns/abbott/100124

[88] (Guindon, 1976, pp. 315, 374)

[89] (Schneiders, 1978, p. 698, col. 2, bottom) Here is the relevant passage: "At the basis of these developments in practice are profound theological convictions about the dignity and equality of persons, the inalienability of personal freedom and responsibility, the right of every individual to justice, **and**

the irreplaceable value for community life of full participation by the members." The last paragraph of the article speaks of the "theological awakening of the 20th century" that "is moving away from an emphasis on... obligations and toward an emphasis on commitment to personal spiritual growth and to participation in the world-transforming mission of the Church." The emphasis on personal growth comes from the influence of humanistic psychology, and we see this same language all throughout *Amoris Laetitia*. Similarly, we see a conspicuous absence of any mention of moral law and obligation in AL.

[90] (Kosnick, Carroll, Cunningham, Modras, & Schulte, 1977, p. 216)

[91] (Kosnick, Carroll, Cunningham, Modras, & Schulte, 1977, p. 216)

[92] (Kosnick, Carroll, Cunningham, Modras, & Schulte, 1977, pp. 53–61)

[93] (Kosnick, Carroll, Cunningham, Modras, & Schulte, 1977, p. 53)

[94] (Francis, 2015) See par. 2, par. 300, and par. 304—especially 304.

[95] (Catholic Resource Network—Trinity Communications, 1994) See Coulson's comments on the Jesuit "Third Way." This was a concoction of the Santa Clara Conference in California in 1967, and it represented a third option between married monogamy

and religious celibacy. In a word, this "Third Way" amounted to a rationalization for fornication, according to Coulson. Coulson blames Rogers's influence on the Jesuits for this innovation. Pope Francis was still in seminary while the Jesuits were in the process of implementing their many psychology-inspired reforms. What was the impact of these reforms on the Jesuits? Becker states that they destroyed the order,

(Becker, The Re-Formed Jesuits, Volume I—A History of Changes in Jesuit Formation During the Decade 1965–1975, 1992, p. 165). As mentioned above, Becker explained how traditional spiritual texts were replaced by works of pop-psychology. Here is his conclusion: "By the end of the 1960s, little of the traditional lifestyle remained. A pattern of living that had been followed for generations—sometimes even for centuries—had largely disappeared over the course of three to four years.... *[M]ost traces of the previous lifestyle had been obliterated.*" Thus, the very same psychology that was responsible for the horrific epidemic of clerical sexual abuse was equally responsible for the destruction of the Jesuit Order according to Becker. Francis seems intent on repeating history. By spreading the very same pseudopsychology that destroyed religious orders and turned priests into child molesters, Francis is spreading these very same errors to the entire Church. The result will be the same, but on a global scale. To borrow from Becker, Francis is "obliterating" the Catholic Church.

A note on Pedro Arrupe, the man in charge of the Jesuits while they were being "obliterated." Bernstein certainly portrays Arrupe as sympathetic to the reform movement—a point that should be remembered as the man's cause for canonization advances under Francis (Bernstein & Politi, 1996, pp. 419–422). In fairness to Arrupe, on the other hand, Becker notes that he condemned the "Third Way" movement in the Society of Jesus (Becker, The Re-Formed Jesuits, Volume I—A History of Changes in Jesuit Formation During the Decade 1965–1975, 1992, p. 72).

[96] (Hickson, 2019) See online: https://www.lifesitenews.com/blogs/evidence-pope-follows-blueprint-to-change-church-by-dissident-cardinal-who-led-st.-gallen-mafia

[97] From *Lumen Gentium* 25:
"Furthermore, when the Roman Pontiff, or the body of bishops together with him, define a doctrine, they make the definition in conformity with revelation itself, to which all are bound to adhere and to which they are obliged to submit.... The Roman Pontiff and the bishops, by reason of their office and the seriousness of the matter, apply themselves with zeal to the work of enquiring by every suitable means into this revelation and of giving apt expression to its contents; they do not, however, admit any new public revelation as pertaining to the divine deposit of faith."

[98] It would seem from the fact that Francis has given us nothing new in *Amoris Laetitia,* that the case for heresy should be a rather simple one. Because AL is nothing more than a regurgitation of the theology of dissent of the seventies, **the ideas in it have already been condemned by a competent authority—John Paul II in Veritatis Splendor.** Nothing more remains to do, then, but to follow through with the proper canonical procedures.

[99] The pope's denigration of the traditional moral law in favor of individualism and relativism is a point of special concern. To be sure, it was a consistent feature of the progressive theology that followed the theories of humanistic psychology. Becker blamed this individualism for breeding a spirit of lawlessness in the Jesuits: (Becker, The Re-Formed Jesuits, Volume I—A History of Changes in Jesuit Formation During the Decade 1965–1975, 1992, pp. 169–174). But lawlessness in a pope is especially incongruous. Certainly St. Paul would agree:

> "Let no one deceive you in any way; for that day will not come, unless the rebellion comes first, and the man of lawlessness is revealed, the son of perdition, who opposes and exalts himself against every so-called god or object of worship, so that he takes his seat in the temple of God, proclaiming himself to be God.... And then the

Confronting the Pope of Suspicion

lawless one will be revealed, and the Lord Jesus will slay him with the breath of his mouth and destroy him by his appearing and his coming. The coming of the lawless one by the activity of Satan will be with all power and with pretended signs and wonders, and with all wicked deception for those who are to perish, because they refused to love the truth and so be saved. Therefore God sends upon them a strong delusion, to make them believe what is false, so that all may be condemned who did not believe the truth but had pleasure in unrighteousness" (2Thess. 2: 3–12, RSVCE).

[100] (CNA Staff, 2016) See online: https://www.catholicnewsagency.com/news/no-doctrine-change-from-pope-francis-but-a-call-for-better-pastoral-care-85474

[101] (Sullins, 2018, pp.27–31)

[102] (Gravino, How Neuroscience Explains Sex Abuse and Vindicates ... Prayer and Fasting, 2018) See online: https://stream.org/how-neuroscience-explains-sex-abuse-and-vindicates-prayer-and-fasting/

[103] (Catholic Resource Network—Trinity Communications, 1994) See online: https://

www.ewtn.com/library/PRIESTS/COULSON.TXT

[104] (Gravino, The Cause of Declining Violence—Enlightenment? Or Incarceration?, 2018) See online: https://newwalden.org/2018/03/14/the-cause-of-declining-violence-enlightenment-or-incarceration/

[105] (John Paul II, Man and Woman He Created Them —A Theology of the Body, 1997, pp. 145–146) See lecture 4, September 26, 1979, paragraphs 4–5, and note 8.

[106] https://betterchurchgovernance.org

[107] According to *Veritatis Splendor* 81, it is a teaching of Sacred Scripture and Tradition that there exist absolute moral norms that govern sexual morality. The Church follows this teaching of divine revelation when it declares adultery, fornication, homosexuality, and other sexual acts outside of marriage and procreation to be intrinsically evil. In the cases of such intrinsically evil acts, there exist no circumstances or situations that can permit or justify them. *Amoris Laetitia* denies this teaching of revelation when it declares in paragraph 304: "It is true that general rules set forth a good which can never be disregarded or neglected, but in their formulation they cannot provide absolutely for all particular situations." In so declaring, AL 304 has denied the existence of absolute moral norms that are true and valid without exception and has thus denied the existence of intrinsic evils. See also note

69, above.

[108] *Confronting the Pope of Suspicion*, p. 37

[109] Some quarters of the Catholic mainstream media (notably CNA) strenuously defended *Amoris Laetitia* against criticism, but those defenses became unsustainable in light of the "December Massacre." Moreover, I showed how some of those defenses rested on faulty interpretations of the *Amoris Laetitia* text: "The Catholic News Agency Misrepresented Key Amoris Text": https://newwalden.org/archives/11360.

[110] "What Is the 'December Massacre'? My Latest Interview with Patrick Coffin": https://newwalden.org/archives/15696

[111] "The German Church Has Fallen—Why Is No One Reporting This?": https://newwalden.org/archives/11371

[112] "Confronting the German Bishops of Suspicion—And the New Protestant Reformation":
https://newwalden.org/archives/13063

[113] "What Is the 'December Massacre'? My Latest Interview with Patrick Coffin": https://newwalden.org/archives/15696

[114] "What Is the 'December Massacre'? My Latest Interview with Patrick Coffin": https://newwalden.org/archives/15696

[115] "The Catholic News Agency Misrepresented Key Amoris Text" https://newwalden.org/archives/11360

[116] https://www.firstthings.com/web-exclusives/2020/02/as-the-synodal-way-begins

[117] https://www.washingtonpost.com/local/a-catholic-case-for-same-sex-marriage/2012/02/13/gIQAl4cwDR_story.html

[118] https://www.wordonfire.org/resources/lecture/on-the-gospel-of-the-family-world-meeting-of-families-2018/5892/. See minutes 28–40 of video.

[119] https://www.wordonfire.org/resources/lecture/on-the-gospel-of-the-family-world-meeting-of-families-2018/5892/. See minutes 40–45 of video.

[120] Perhaps the best way to understand the meaning of "ideal" in the sexual liberation heresy is by way of illustration. Consider this statement from the *New Catholic Encyclopedia* article on religious vows:

> "Without denying that the consecration constituted by religious profession is *ideally* life-long and that definitive commitment is possible and life-enhancing *for those whose gift it is*, there is increasing discussion of the possibility that not every religious profession need be perpetual." NCE,

Confronting the Pope of Suspicion

p. 697

One can infer from the passage that "ideally" means "considered in the abstract, without reference to concrete situations and circumstances." One can also infer that such ideal norms are not valid apart from a consideration of those situations and circumstances. Only people who meet certain subjective criteria—those "whose gift it is"—have an obligation to make their vows perpetual. That this is where this passage is going is illustrated by a passage from another heretical text, *Human Sexuality*:

> "The third level of moral evaluation consists of more concrete norms, rules, precepts, or guidelines.... To the extent that they refer to concrete, physical actions (e.g., masturbation, sterilization, contraception, premarital sex) without specifying particular circumstances or intention, to that extent they cannot be regarded as universal and absolute moral norms.
> These norms indicate what Christian experience has proven to occur generally.... Exceptions may occur.... Because such norms are not universal moral absolutes, we have chosen to refer to these more concrete formulations as "guidelines." *Human Sexuality*, p. 97

The heretics maintained that the condemnation of sexual immorality in the Bible depended on abstract, universal principles—*ideals*—that did not account for particular situations and circumstances that the heretics claimed were essential for determining a binding moral obligation. And for this neglectful oversight on the part of the Gospel writers, such *ideals* or universal principles which they impart to us are in fact, invalid, according to the heretics. To be valid and binding, a moral principle must account for important factors, which include, among other things, the psychological facts of the moral agent in question. Such psychological facts will vary from person to person, and this variation is decisive in determining whether a moral obligation can be binding. For example, the sexual liberation heretics argued that the moral condemnation of homosexuality in the Bible did not apply to persons of a certain "psycho-sexual" constitution who exhibited same-sex attraction. To be blunt, gay people could freely ignore Biblical condemnations of homosexuality. Pope John Paul II condemned this critique of Biblical morality in *Veritatis Splendor.*

[121] *Human Sexuality*, p. 216

[122] *Human Sexuality*, p. 59

[123] https://www.lifesitenews.com/blogs/pope-francis-declares-2021-will-be-year-dedicated-to-error-filled-amoris-laetitia

[124] I make the point very clear in CPS that there is doctrinal change all over the place in *Amoris Laeti-*

tia. In paragraph 3, he endorses a form of cultural relativism that doesn't get developed in Amoris at all. He waited for *Querida Amazonia* to do that. As I explain in the article "*Querida Amazonia*—The Good, the Bad, and the Ugly Polyhedron of Perversion," the Francis version of cultural relativism means that Church doctrine may vary from culture to culture: https://newwalden.org/archives/14055. See also: "What Did Theologians Teach About Pedophilia? (Part 2)—The Francis Connection": https://newwalden.org/archives/9183.

[125] https://www.wordonfire.org/resources/lecture/on-the-gospel-of-the-family-world-meeting-of-families-2018/5892/. See minutes 40–45 of video.

[126] https://en.wikipedia.org/wiki/Robert_Barron

[127] *Confronting the Pope of Suspicion*

[128] https://en.wikipedia.org/wiki/Robert_Barron Barron was a student at Mundelein in 1986, and Cunningham taught there for 24 years, from 1967–1991: http://www.sscm-usa.org/1-agnes_cunningham.html.

[129] *Human Sexuality*, p. 216

[130] *Goodbye, Good Men*, chapter 4

[131] *Goodbye, Good Men*, chapter 4

[132] Since the publication of *Amoris Laetitia*, Fr.

James Martin has called for the elimination of language in the Catechism that describes homosexuality as disordered. This is a clear step in the direction of gay equality. And now the Germans are joining the movement.

[133] Consider, for example, what it means for the German bishops to say that homosexuality is normal and that we need a scientific understanding of sexuality. Does that sound like they are preserving the teaching that homosexuality is sinful? The concept of sin, itself, is hardly a scientific concept. And what does Fr. James Martin mean, exactly, when he says he looks forward to the day when gay couples can kiss at the sign of peace? Ask yourself this important question: if gays can kiss at the sign of peace, what are they allowed to do at communion time? As I stated in CPS, it was a central issue of the sexual liberation heresy that gays should be allowed to receive Holy Communion. See: "The Cost of Doing Nothing (about Fr. James Martin), Part 1": https://newwalden.org/archives/3283

[134] *Confronting the Pope of Suspicion.* See also "What Did Theologians Teach About Pedophilia?": https://newwalden.org/archives/8260.

[135] "Scandal Time (Continued)" *First Things.* https://www.firstthings.com/article/2002/06/scandal-time-continued

[136] I do not belong in the camp that claims that the term "heresy" is a technical canon law term.

Confronting the Pope of Suspicion

We know one when we see one. The Doctors and Fathers of the Church were condemning heresies long before canon law was systematized.

[137] The heretics are probably not denying the existence of minimum standards for a state of grace and admission to Holy Communion. They probably would agree that an unrepentant Jack the Ripper fails to meet that standard. But they somehow claim competence in moving the goalposts. What grants them this competence? The Bible does not grant them such authority (Gal. 1: 8). Surely, *science* is not competent to judge who is in a state of grace or mortal sin. It looks like just plain narcissism to assert that your favorite sins are actually not so bad in God's eyes after all.

[138] Bishop Barron wrote a book about the clergy sexual abuse scandal, *Letter to a Suffering Church*. He neglected to mention that bad theologians defended pedophilia and encouraged priests and seminarians to be sexual and experimental.

[139] *Goodbye, Good Men*, Introduction. Now consider for a moment this curiosity. If Mundelein actively persecuted anyone who challenged the dominant gay liberation culture, ask yourself how it was that Barron managed to get promoted from professor to rector.

[140] https://www.lifesitenews.com/news/breaking-vatican-rejects-blessings-for-homosexual-couples

[141] https://reason.com/2015/04/02/was-memories-pizza-a-victim-of-irrespons/ See also: https://www.nationalreview.com/2017/11/masterpiece-cakeshop-case-stop-misrepresenting/

[142] https://www.ncregister.com/cna/german-catholic-bishops-call-for-change-to-catechism-on-homosexuality

[143] https://www.ncregister.com/cna/brazilian-bishops-discuss-controversial-text-of-ecumenical-lenten-campaign

[144] https://www.katholisch.de/artikel/29080-marx-kirche-darf-uebergang-in-naechste-epoche-nicht-versaeumen. See also: "What Is the 'December Massacre'? My Latest Interview with Patrick Coffin": https://newwalden.org/archives/15696

[145] For history of the LGBT movement at St. Francis in Raleigh, see: https://drive.google.com/file/d/1ky59hNzYDCyal1Z9q8g1VV9c-mXtTzUX/view See also: https://www.stfrancisraleigh.org/lgbt/

[146] "Is Boycotting Immoral?": https://newwalden.org/archives/4111

[147] One of the activist clergy in Raleigh behind this movement delivered a pro-inclusion homily a couple of years ago in which he described those who oppose inclusion as "diabolical." That's what the

lay faithful are facing—a venomous dehumanization that will rationalize any means to crush opposition to the gay apostasy.

[148] https://www.wordonfire.org/resources/lecture/on-the-gospel-of-the-family-world-meeting-of-families-2018/5892/. See minutes 35–45 of video.

[149] https://stream.org/if-hillary-wins-solzhenitsyns-action-plan/

Made in the USA
Coppell, TX
18 September 2022